SUMMER BRAIN QUEST

Dear Parent,

At Brain Quest, we believe learning should be an adventure—a *quest* for knowledge. Our mission has always been to guide children on that quest, to keep them excited, motivated, and curious, and to give them the confidence they need to do well in school. Now, we're extending the quest to summer! Meet SUMMER BRAIN QUEST: It's a workbook. It's a game. It's an outdoor adventure. And it's going to stop summer slide!

Research shows that if kids take a break from learning all summer, they can lose up to three months' worth of knowledge from the previous grade. So we set out to create a one-of-a-kind workbook experience that delivers personalized learning for every kind of kid. Personalized learning is an educational method where exercises are tailored to each child's strengths, needs, and interests. Our goal was to empower kids to have a voice in what and how they learned during the summer, while ensuring they get enough practice of the fundamentals. The result: SUMMER BRAIN QUEST—a complete interactive program that is easy to use and designed to engage each unique kid all summer long.

So how does it work? Each SUMMER BRAIN QUEST WORKBOOK includes a pullout tri-fold map that functions as a game board, progress chart, and personalized learning system. Our map shows different routes that correspond to 110 pages of curriculum-based exercises and 8 outdoor learning experiences. The variety of routes enables kids to choose different topics and activities while guaranteeing practice in weaker skills. We've also included over 150 stickers to mark progress, incentivize challenging exercises, and celebrate accomplishments. As kids complete activities and earn stickers, they can put them wherever they like on the map, so each child's map is truly unique—just like your kid. To top it all off, we included a Summer Brainiac Award to mark your child's successful completion of his or her quest. SUMMER BRAIN QUEST guides kids so they feel supported, and it offers positive feedback and builds confidence by showing kids how far they've come and just how much they've learned.

Each SUMMER BRAIN QUEST WORKBOOK has been created in consultation with an award-winning teacher specializing in that grade. We cover the core competencies of reading, writing, and math, as well as the essentials of social studies and science. We ensure that our exercises are aligned to Common Core State Standards, Next Generation Science Standards, and state social studies standards.

Loved by kids and adored by teachers, Brain Quest is America's #1 educational bestseller and has been an important bridge to the classroom for millions of children. SUMMER BRAIN QUEST is an effective new tool for parents, homeschoolers, tutors, and teachers alike to stop summer slide. By providing fun, personalized, and meaningful educational materials, our mission is to help ALL kids keep their skills ALL summer long. Most of all, we want kids to know:

It's your summer. It's your workbook. It's your learning adventure.

—The editors of Brain Quest

This book belongs to:

_____

Library of Congress Cataloging-in-Publication Data is available.

ISBN 978-0-7611-8916-9

Summer Series Concept by Nathalie Le Du, Daniel Nayeri, Tim Hall
Writers   Megan Hewes Butler, Claire Piddock
Consulting Editor   Kimberly Oliver Burnim
Art Director   Colleen AF Venable
Cover, Map, Sticker, and Additional Character Illustrator   Edison Yan
Illustrator   Maris Wicks
Series Designer   Tim Hall
Editor   Nathalie Le Du
Production Editor   Jessica Rozler
Production Manager   Julie Primavera

Workman books are available at special discounts when purchased in bulk for premiums and sales promotions as well as for fund-raising or educational use. Special editions or book excerpts can also be created to specification. For details, contact the Special Sales Director at the address below, or send an email to specialmarkets@workman.com.

DISCLAIMER
The publisher and authors disclaim responsibility for any loss, injury, or damages caused as a result of any of the instructions described in this book.

Workman Publishing Co., Inc.
225 Varick Street
New York, NY 10014-4381
workman.com

BRAIN QUEST, IT'S FUN TO BE SMART!, and WORKMAN are
registered trademarks of Workman Publishing Co., Inc.

Printed in China
First printing March 2017

10 9 8 7 6 5 4 3 2

SUMMER BRAIN QUEST

BETWEEN GRADES K&1

For adventurers ages 5–6

Written by Megan Hewes Butler and Claire Piddock
Consulting Editor: Kimberly Oliver Burnim

WORKMAN PUBLISHING
NEW YORK

4

Contents

Your Quest

Your quest is to sticker as many paths on the map as possible and reach the final destination by the end of summer to become an official Summer Brainiac.

Basic Components

Summer progress map

100+ pages of quest exercises

110 quest stickers

8 Outside Quests

8 Outside Quest stickers

Over 40 achievement stickers

Summer Brainiac Award

100% sticker

Setup

Detach the map and place it on a flat surface.

Begin at **START** on your map.

How to Play

To advance along a path, you must complete a quest exercise with the matching color and symbol. For example:

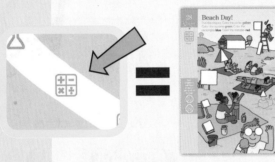 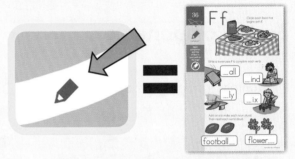

Math exercise from the orange level (Level 2)

English language arts exercise from the red level (Level 3)

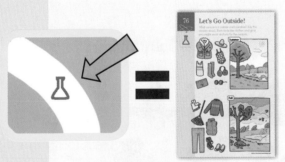 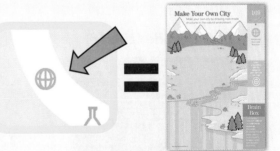

Science exercise from the blue level (Level 6)

Social studies exercise from the green level (Level 7)

If you complete the challenge, you earn a matching quest sticker.

Place the quest sticker on the path to continue on your journey.

At the end of each level, you earn an achievement sticker.

Apply it to the map and move on to the next level!

Outside Quests

Throughout the map, you will encounter paths that lead to Outside Quests.

To advance along those paths, you must complete one of the Outside Quests.

If you complete an Outside Quest, you earn an Outside Quest sticker and advance toward 100% completion!

Bonuses

If you complete a bonus question, you earn an achievement sticker.

BONUS: Plants grow from seeds. Draw some seeds in the soil to grow more plants!

→ Then add this sticker to your map!

Subject Completion

If you complete all of the quest exercises in a subject (math, English language arts, science, or social studies), you earn an achievement sticker.

CONGRATULATIONS! You completed all of your science quests! You earned:

Summer Brain Quest Completion Sticker and Award

If you complete your quest, you earn a Summer Brain Quest completion sticker and award!

100% Sticker

Sticker *every* possible route and finish *all* the Outside Quests to earn the 100% sticker!

Level 1

Alphabet

Ready for Takeoff!

Read the alphabet aloud, and fill in the missing uppercase letters.

Upon completion, add this sticker to your path on the map!

Desert Digits

Trace the numbers in the sand.
Then circle your age.

Writing
Numbers

1 2 3

4 5 6

7 8 9

Upon
completion,
add this
sticker to
your path on
the map!

Train Travel

Read the train's directions. Then draw a line on the tracks to help the train find the treasure.

Maps

Upon completion, add this sticker to your path on the map!

Go UP to the cactus.
Travel BEHIND the mountains.
Make a RIGHT before the sand castle.
End your trip BETWEEN the shovels!

START

END

Dressing for the Desert

The camel is going on a trip through the hot, dry desert. Say the word for each picture, and cross out the items he will NOT need to pack for this weather.

Weather

Upon completion, add this sticker to your path on the map!

BONUS: Write or draw a picture of what you wear when the weather is hot.

Hat

Then add this sticker to your map!

Storytelling

Welcome Home!

The Gila woodpecker lives in a desert cactus. Write or draw about what happens when he gets to his home. What might he find there? What might he do there?

Upon completion, add these stickers to your path on the map!

Then add this sticker to your map!

Nest

BONUS: Write the word "cactus."

Cactus.

Counting

Hide-and-Seek

Count the number of each animal. Then write the number.

owls

butterflies

5 rabbits

Upon completion, add these stickers to your path on the map!

6
hawks

2
rams

3
deer

tortoise

4
toads

7
geckos

BONUS: Find the sticks that form a number. What number is it?

4

How many sticks form the number?

4

Then add this sticker to your map!

Search for Shadows

The sun is shining, and it's hot in the desert. Animals need shade and water to survive. Draw a line to help the camel to the cool oasis.

Upon completion, add this sticker to your path on the map!

Level 1 complete!

Add this achievement sticker
to your path...

...and move on to

Level 2!

A a

Alphabet: A

Color each apple with **A** or **a**.

Write an uppercase **A** to complete each word.

April August America

The word **hat** has a **short a** sound. Circle each object that also has a **short a** sound.

Let's Get Digging!

Draw a line to match each community helper with his or her tools.

Upon completion, add this sticker to your path on the map!

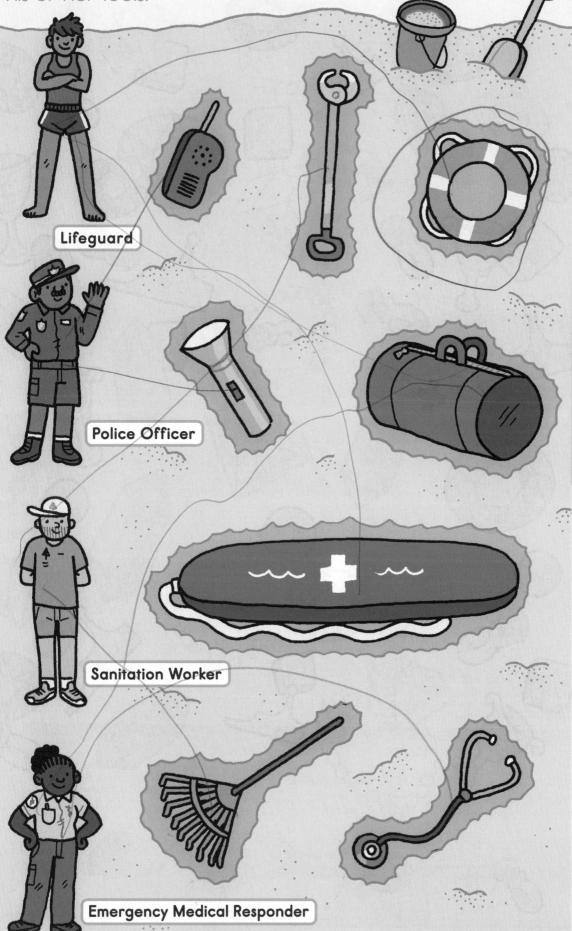

Lifeguard

Police Officer

Sanitation Worker

Emergency Medical Responder

Treasure Hunt!

Count the number of each type of treasure. Then write the number.

Counting

Upon completion, add these stickers to your path on the map!

Then add this sticker to your map!

BONUS: Draw your own gems. Then write the number of gems you drew.

Summer Brain Quest: Between Grades K & 1

Let's Swim!

The ocean is a saltwater habitat.
Read the names and color the animals
that live in the ocean!

Ocean
Habitats

Upon
completion,
add this
sticker to
your path on
the map!

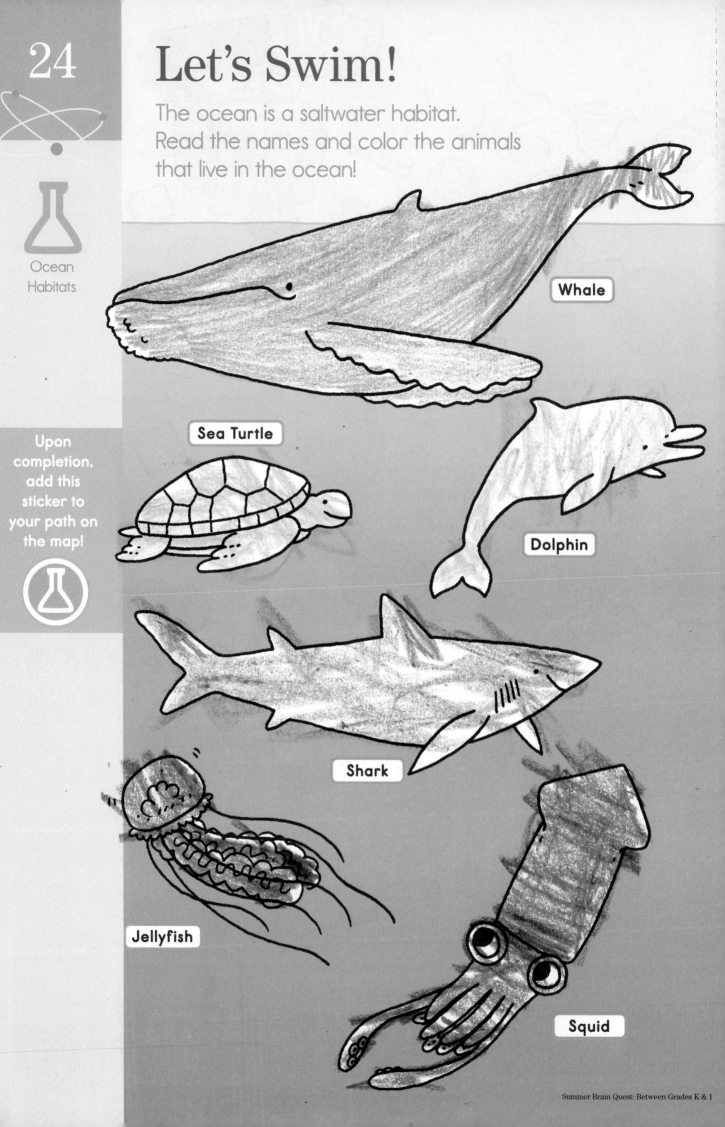

Whale

Sea Turtle

Dolphin

Shark

Jellyfish

Squid

Coyote Chase

Look at each picture. What happens first, second, third, and last? Draw a line to match each event to the correct order on the timeline.

Making a Timeline

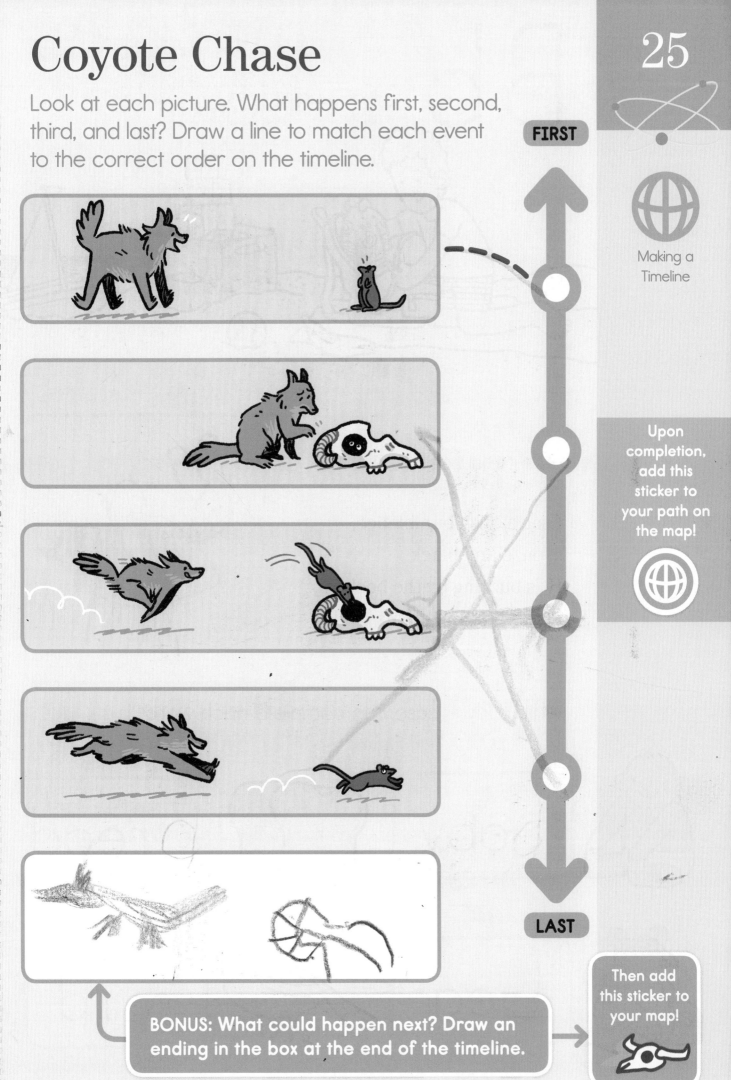

FIRST

LAST

Upon completion, add this sticker to your path on the map!

Then add this sticker to your map!

BONUS: What could happen next? Draw an ending in the box at the end of the timeline.

B b

Alphabet: B

Color each object that begins with **b**.

Draw a picture about the poem.

I see a busy bumblebee,
bronze and black.
He's buzzing by the beehive,
wings buzzing on his back.

Write a lowercase **b** to complete each word.

  baby

  bread

  bear

bird

Cc

Circle the crabs and clams.

Alphabet: C

Write a lowercase **c** to complete each word in each word family.

rat, bat, **c**at

now, plow, **c**ow

map, snap, **c**ap

Upon completion, add this sticker to your path on the map!

Trace the sentence. Capitalize the first letter of the first word of the sentence.

I see a colorful clam on the coral.

Shapes

Beach Day!

Find the shapes. Color the circles **yellow**.
Color the squares **green**. Color the
rectangles **blue**. Color the triangles **red**.

Upon
completion,
add these
stickers to
your path on
the map!

Shapes

BONUS: Draw a shape. Then color it to look like something you might find at a beach.

Then add this sticker to your map!

Dd

Circle each animal that begins with **d**.

Draw a picture about the poem.

The dizzy dizzy dump truck
dumped his load of dirt.
It landed on the driver,
but at least he wasn't hurt!

dumps dirt on driver

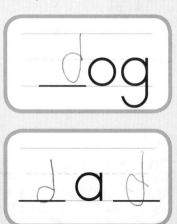

Upon completion, add this sticker to your path on the map!

Write a lowercase **d** to complete each word.

day

dog

did

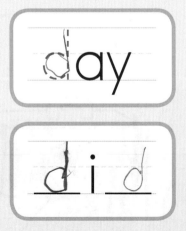
dad

Level 2 complete!

Add this achievement sticker
to your path…

…and move on to

Level

3!

Map Your Neighborhood

Make a map of your neighborhood. First draw your home. Next draw the places that are near your home. If you have room, draw the places that are far away from your home.

Drawing a Map

Upon completion, add this sticker to your path on the map!

Brain Box

Maps can include places where people live, like houses or apartment buildings. Maps can also include places of business, like grocery stores, post offices, and restaurants. Maps can include other details, like roads, train tracks, and rivers too!

BONUS: Add natural elements from your neighborhood, like trees and ponds.

Then add this sticker to your map!

E e

Circle each segment with lowercase **e**.

Alphabet: E

The word **net** has a **short e** sound. Circle each object that also has a **short e** sound.

Upon completion, add this sticker to your path on the map!

Fill in each missing **e** to complete each **long e** word.

b e e

l e a f

t r e e

Shapes

Game On!

Draw a line to match each shape with its name.

Upon completion, add this sticker to your path on the map!

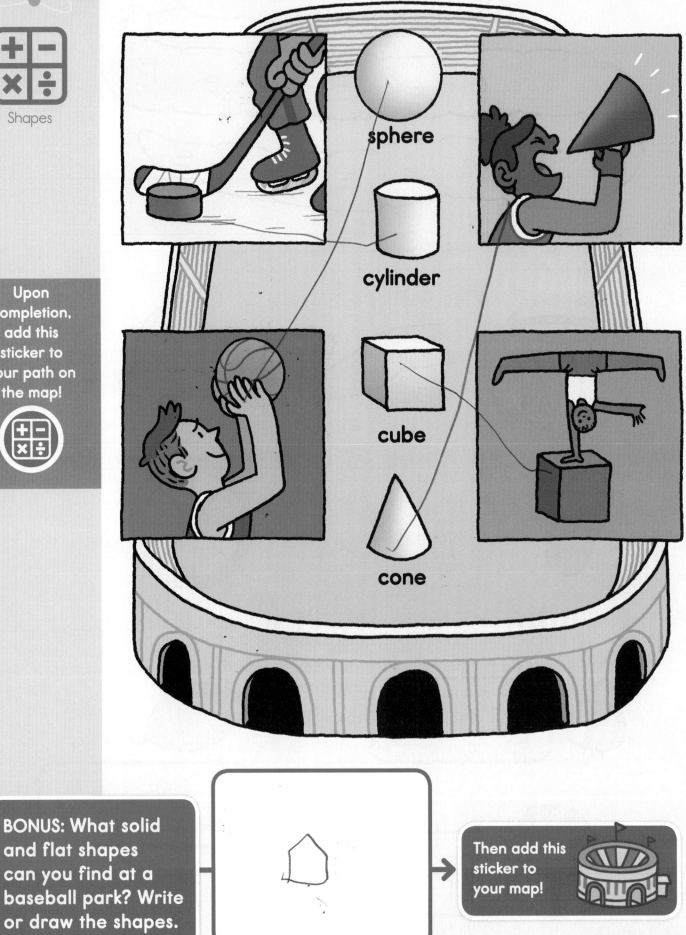

sphere

cylinder

cube

cone

BONUS: What solid and flat shapes can you find at a baseball park? Write or draw the shapes.

Then add this sticker to your map!

Make a Match

Draw on the right what is missing from each animal home on the left.

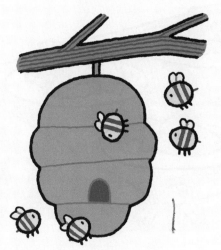
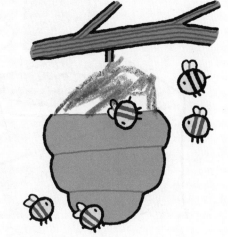

Upon
completion,
add this
sticker to
your path on
the map!

Alphabet: F

F f

Circle each food that begins with **f**.

Write a lowercase **f** to complete each verb.

fall

find

fly

fix

Add an **s** to make each noun plural. Then read each word aloud.

football**s**

flower**s**

G g

Color all of the golf balls, golf carts, and gophers.

Alphabet: G

Write a lowercase **g** to complete each word in each word family.

boat, coat, _g_oat

drum, hum, _g_um

date, late, _g_ate

Add an **s** to make each noun plural. Then read each word aloud.

girl_s_

game_s_

Anthill Map

Read the map key. Color each entrance **green**. Color each nursery **red**. Color each food storage room **orange**. Color the queen's room yellow. Color the rest area **blue**.

Map Key

Entrance

Nursery

Food Storage Room

Queen's Room

Rest Area

Reduce, Reuse, Recycle!

Draw how you could reuse each box.

Recycling

Upon completion, add this sticker to your path on the map!

Brain Box

One way to help the environment is to reuse things instead of throwing them away.

Flat or Solid

Color all the shapes. Then draw a circle around the flat shapes and a square around the solid shapes.

cone

ORDER HERE

circle

rectangle

square

cube

triangle

Hh

Circle each object that begins with **h**.

Trace the sentence. Capitalize the first letter of the first word of the sentence.

Look at the hair on the horses' heads.

Write a lowercase **h** to complete each verb.

hold

hurt

help

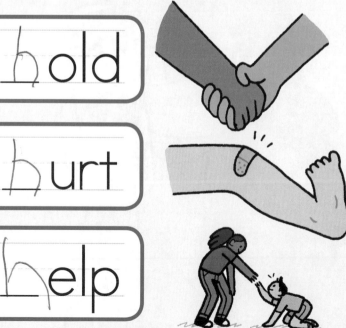

I i

Circle each lowercase letter **i**.

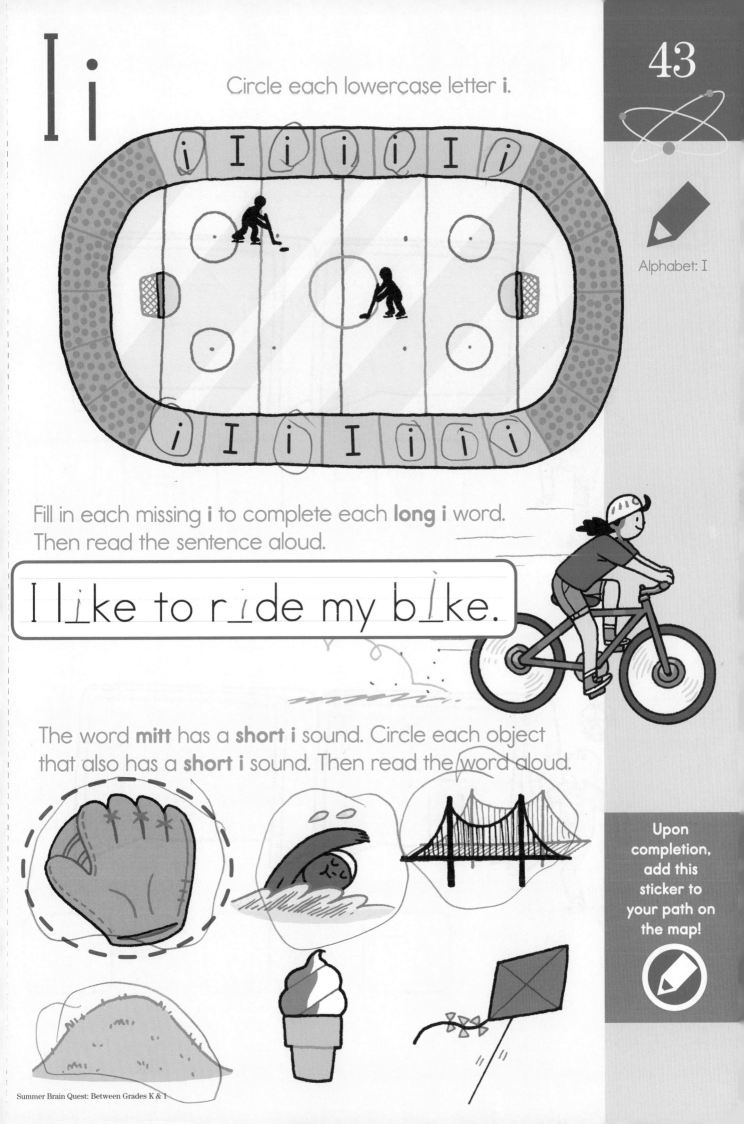

Fill in each missing **i** to complete each **long i** word. Then read the sentence aloud.

I like to ride my bike.

The word **mitt** has a **short i** sound. Circle each object that also has a **short i** sound. Then read the word aloud.

Upon completion, add this sticker to your path on the map!

Summer Brain Quest: Between Grades K & 1

Addition

Goal!

Draw 10 soccer balls in the left net. Then draw the missing balls in the right net to match the total. Next trace the equation.

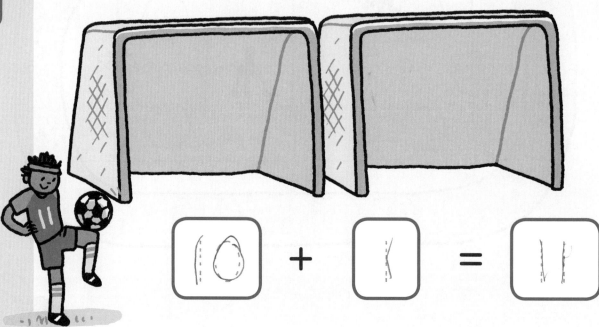

$$10 + 1 = 11$$

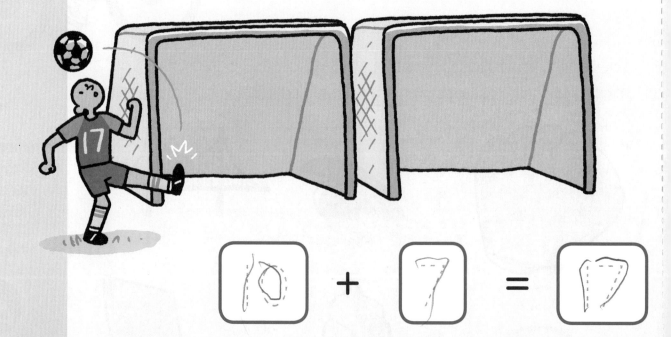

$$10 + 7 = 17$$

Addition

$10 + 5 = 15$

$10 + 9 = 19$

Upon completion, add these stickers to your path on the map!

$10 + 3 = 13$

Let's Go Shopping!

Neighborhoods

HARDWARE

TOYS!

BOOKSTORE

SHOES

Shopping List
- Books
- Ballet Slippers
- Bananas
- Hammer
- Flowers

Match each item on the shopping list to the store where you can buy it.

GROCERY

FLORIST

Upon completion, add this sticker to your path on the map!

BONUS: Draw a place where you can buy ice cream next to the grocery store. It can be a store, a stand, or a truck!

→ Then add this sticker to your map!

Level 3 complete!

Add this achievement sticker
to your path...

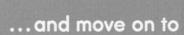

...and move on to

Level

4!

Draw Your Own Plant

A plant has parts that help it grow.
Draw your own plant and label the parts.

Plant Parts

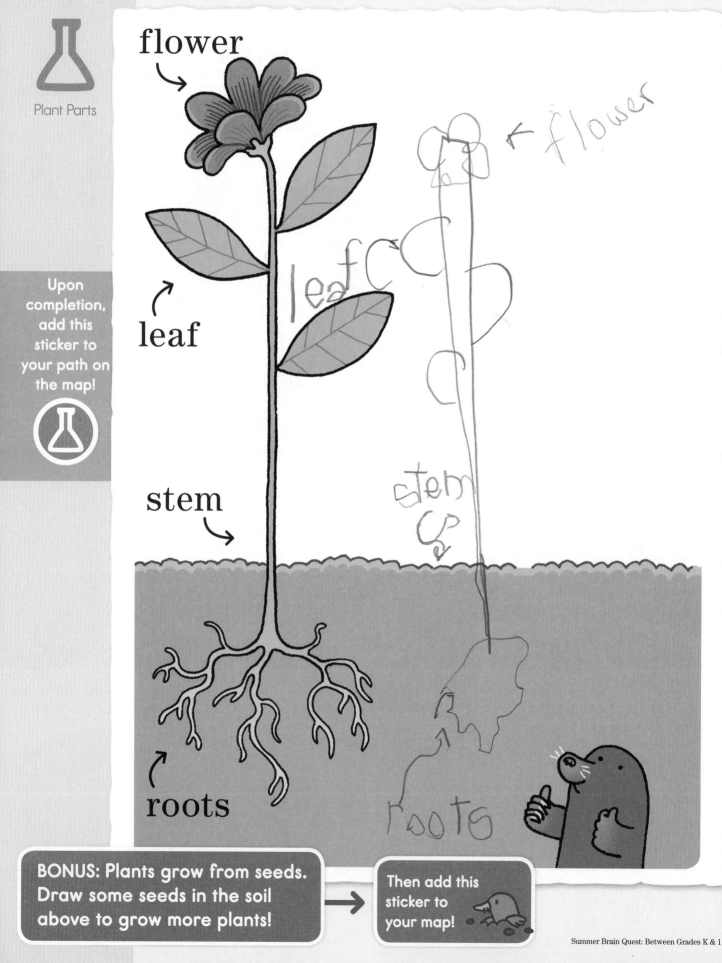

flower

leaf

stem

roots

BONUS: Plants grow from seeds. Draw some seeds in the soil above to grow more plants! → **Then add this sticker to your map!**

More Animals!

Count the animals in each group and write the number. Then circle which group has more.

Compare

Upon completion, add this sticker to your path on the map!

BONUS: Circle the group that has the most animals.

Then add this sticker to your map!

2

3

3

6

4

5

Natural Resources

Draw living natural resources to complete the farm.

Living and
Nonliving
Things

BONUS: Draw a farmer using a nonliving and a living natural resource. → **Then add this sticker to your map!**

Living and
Nonliving
Things

Upon
completion,
add these
stickers to
your path on
the map!

Brain Box

Natural resources are all of the living and nonliving things in nature that we use to help us live. Plants and animals are examples of **living resources**. Dirt, rocks, and water are examples of **nonliving resources**.

Alphabet: J

Jj

Color all of the jaguar's jars of jelly.

Write an uppercase **J** to complete each word.

Janury | June | July

Write a lowercase **j** to complete each verb.
Then read each verb aloud.

Jump

Jog

K k

Color each kite with **K** or **k**.

Alphabet: K

Upon completion, add this sticker to your path on the map!

Write a lowercase **k** to complete each verb.

Kick

Keep

Kiss

Add an **s** to make each noun plural.
Then read each word aloud.

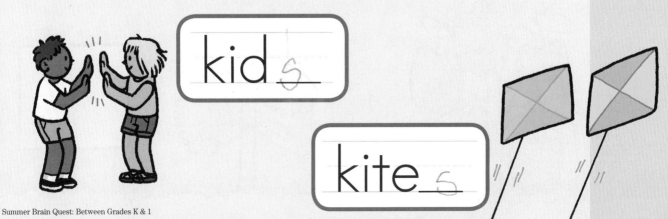

kids

kite s

Addition

Growing Groups

Count each group of vegetables.
Then write the sum in the box.

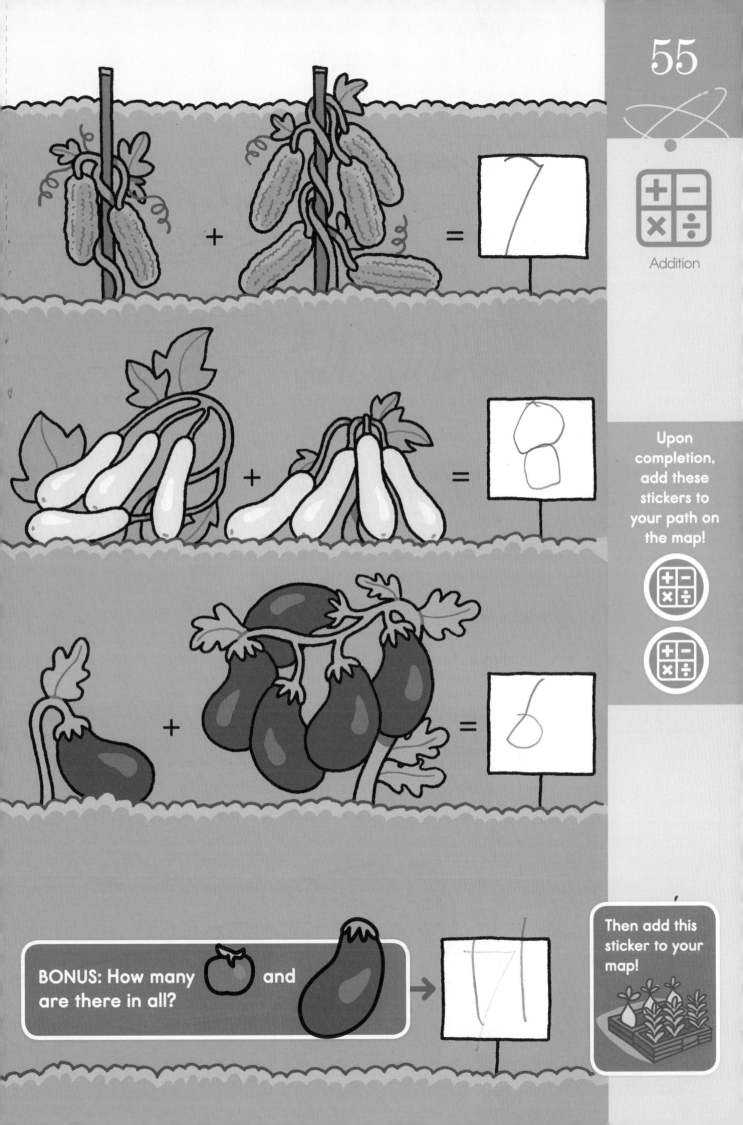

Addition

Upon completion, add these stickers to your path on the map!

BONUS: How many 🍅 and 🍆 are there in all?

Then add this sticker to your map!

L l

Alphabet: L

Upon completion, add this sticker to your path on the map!

Color each object that begins with **l**.

Draw a picture about the poem.

The lost lightning bug leaped
and landed in the lake tonight.
It's dark beneath the water
but he won't turn on his light.

BONUS: Look at the picture and write each word that begins with "l."

Then add this sticker to your map!

Level 4 complete!

Add this achievement sticker
to your path…

…and move on to

Level

5!

Alphabet: M

Mm

Circle each object that begins with **m**.

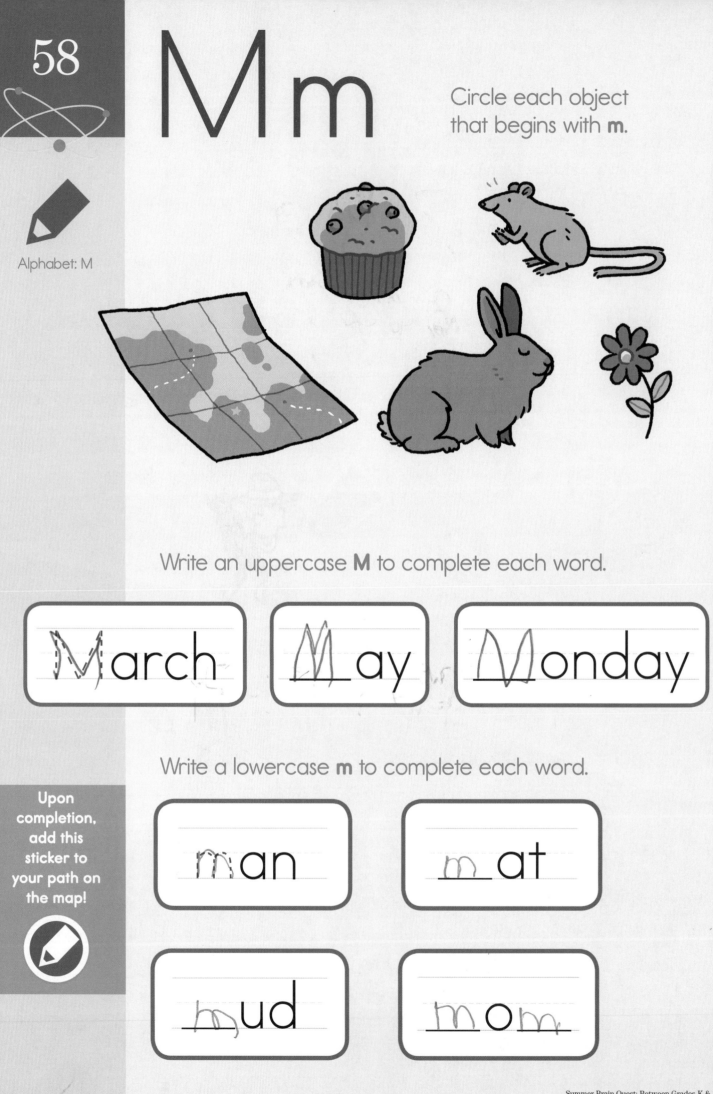

Write an uppercase **M** to complete each word.

| March | May | Monday |

Write a lowercase **m** to complete each word.

man

mat

mud

mom

Flower Power

Draw flowers to show the total, then write the total in the box.

$$\begin{array}{r} 3 \\ +4 \\ \hline \end{array}$$

7

$$\begin{array}{r} 2 \\ +6 \\ \hline \end{array}$$

6

$$\begin{array}{r} 4 \\ +5 \\ \hline \end{array}$$

9

Plant Growth

Let's Get Growing!

The seeds in the soil have the water and sunlight they need to grow. Draw what they will grow into!

Upon completion, add this sticker to your path on the map!

PUMPKIN

SUNFLOWER

APPLE TREE

BONUS: These plants get water from a watering can. Draw another way that plants can get water above.

→ Then add this sticker to your map!

Time for School!

Draw a line to help the girl through her morning routine on her way to school. Describe each step aloud.

Upon completion, add this sticker to your path on the map!

Brain Quest Elementary School

N n

Color each nut with an uppercase **N**.

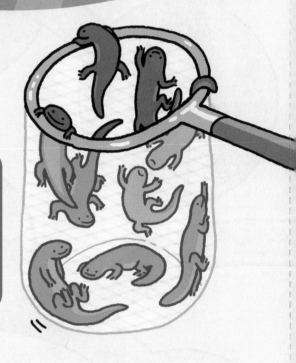

Trace the sentence. Capitalize the first letter of the first word of the sentence.

There are nine newls in the net.

Write a lowercase **n** to complete each word.

night

nail

nest

O o

Circle each owl egg with **O** or **o**.

Alphabet: O

The word **moth** has a **short o** sound. Circle each object that also has a **short o** sound.

Upon completion, add this sticker to your path on the map!

Fill in each missing **o** to complete each **short** and **long o** word. Then read the sentences aloud.

Oh no! The dog lost his bone.

Fly Your Flag!

American Flag

Upon completion, add this sticker to your path on the map!

Color the American flag.

Next, draw a flag to represent your family!

Brain Box

July 4th is **Independence Day**. In 1776 the 13 original colonies declared themselves a new nation, the United States of America. The American flag is the national flag of the United States of America. There are 13 stripes (one for each original colony) and 50 stars (one for each state).

P p

Color each object that begins with **p**.

Write a lowercase **p** to complete each word.

pig

pop

pat

pup

Draw a picture about the poem.

The pretty pig and pink piglet
paddled past the park.
What a peaceful plan they picked,
until they saw a shark!

Forest Habitat

Animals of the Forest
Color the coniferous forest.

Upon completion, add these stickers to your path on the map!

bat

owl

deer

black bear

Brain Box

There are many types of forests. A **coniferous forest** has evergreen trees, which have green needles all year!

Forest
Habitat

vulture

squirrel

woodpecker

wolf

BONUS: Evergreen
trees are called
conifers because
cones grow on
their branches.
The cones contain
seeds! Draw cones
on this branch.

Then add
this sticker
to your
map!

Night Animals!

Count the animals in each group. Write the numbers and the total.

1 + 4 = 5

4 + 3 = 7

3 + 3 = 6

Addition

7 + 2 = 9

Upon completion, add these stickers to your path on the map!

2 + 3 = 5

Then add this sticker to your map!

BONUS: Draw one more raccoon in the group above. Now how many raccoons are there in all?

Addition

Animals of the Meadow

Draw the missing animals to make a group of 10.
Then write the numbers that add to 10.

Upon completion, add this sticker to your path on the map!

9 + 1 = 10

5 + 5 = 10

7 + = 10

Level 5 complete!

Add this achievement sticker
to your path...

...and move on to

Level 6!

Q q

Alphabet: Q

Write **quack** for each quacking duck.

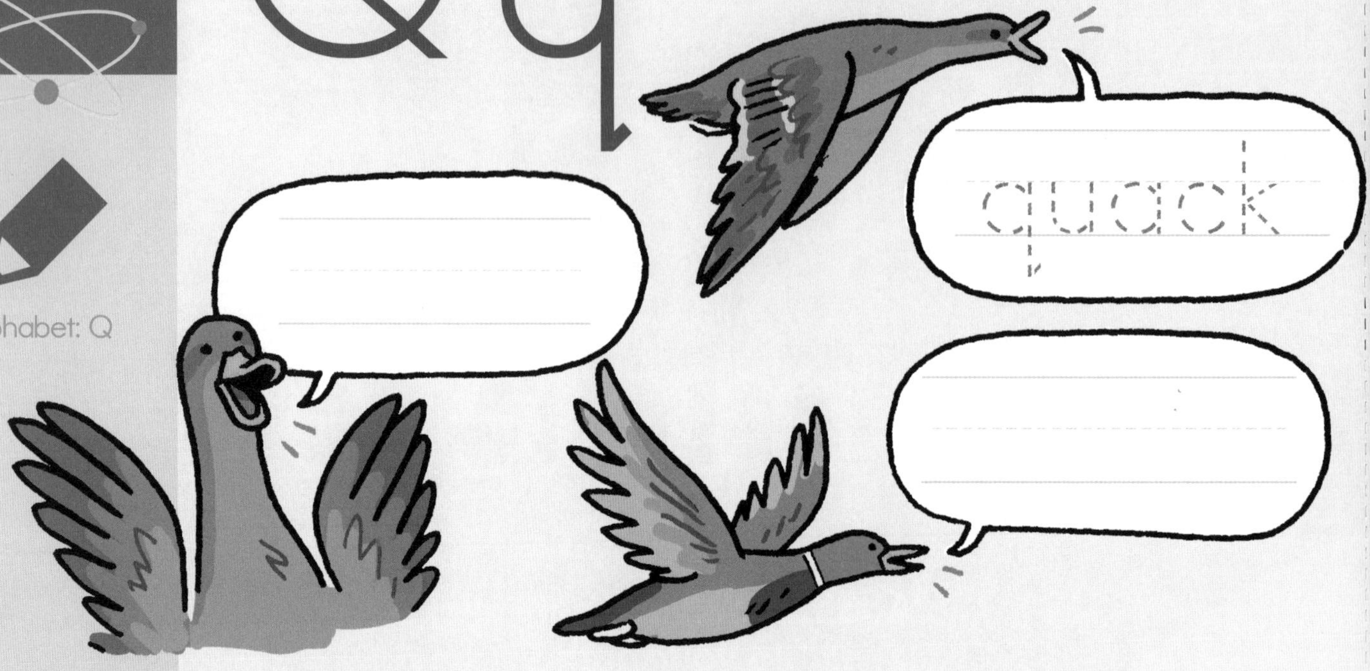

quack

Write a lowercase **q** to complete each noun.

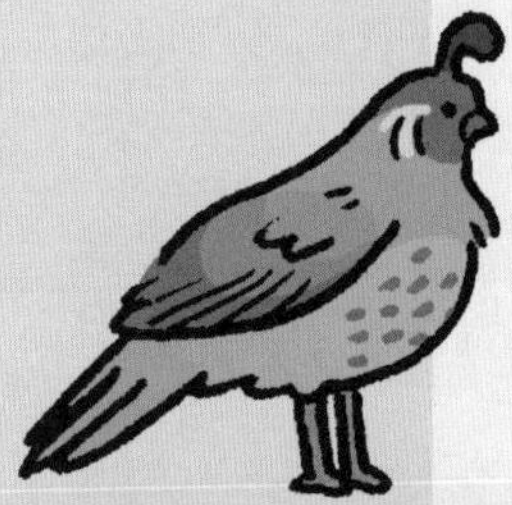

__uail

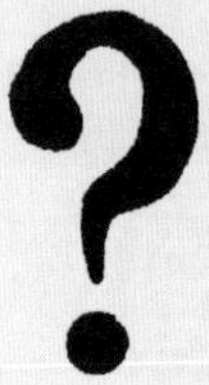

?

__uestion

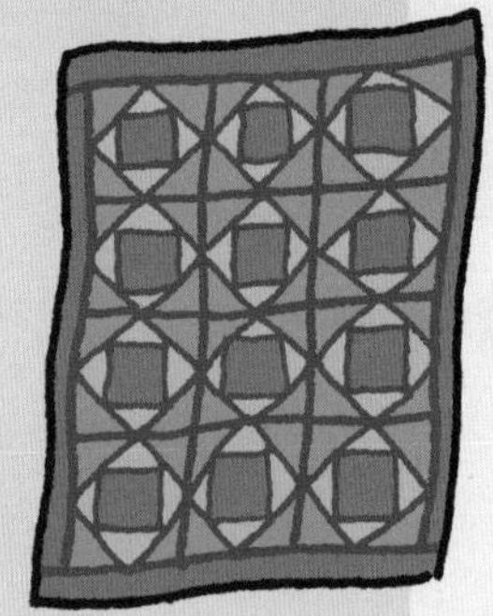

__uilt

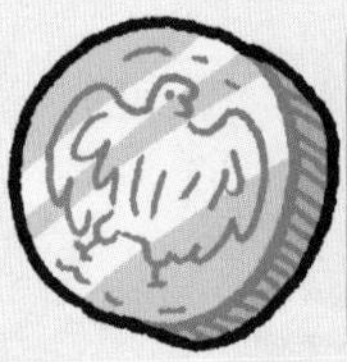

__uarter

Add an **s** to make each noun plural.
Then read each noun aloud.

quart__

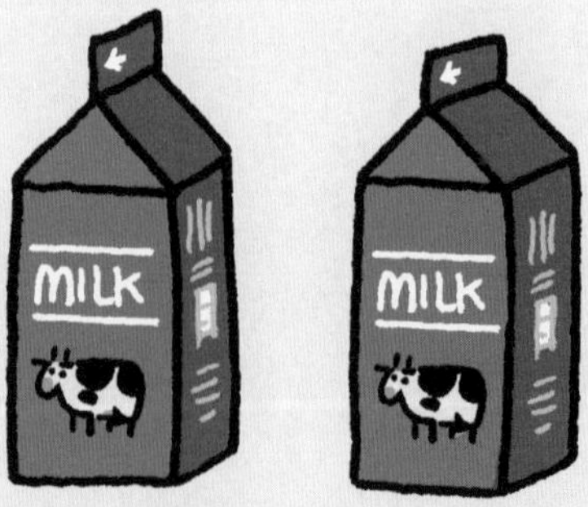

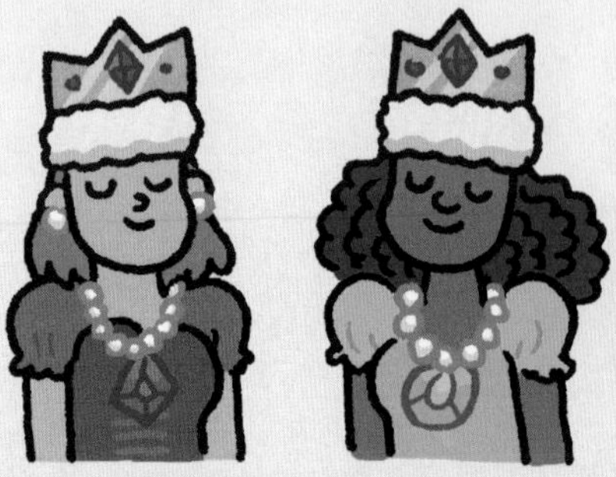

queen__

Changing with Time

PAST

PRESENT

Past, Present, and Future

FUTURE

Imagine how you might travel in the future. Draw a picture of your vehicle.

Upon completion, add this sticker to your path on the map!

BONUS: The way people used fire a long time ago is different from how we use fire now. Write or draw how people used fire in the past.

Then add this sticker to your map!

Brain Box

The way people traveled a long time ago is different from how we travel now. About 200 years ago, people traveled by wagon and horse. Now, people travel in cars, buses, trucks, planes, trains, and more.

Subtraction

Marshmallow Math

Count the marshmallows. Color the number that are burned in black. Write the number of marshmallows that are not burned.

3 are burned. How many are not burned?

4 are burned. How many are not burned?

2 are burned. How many are not burned?

4 are burned.
How many are not burned?

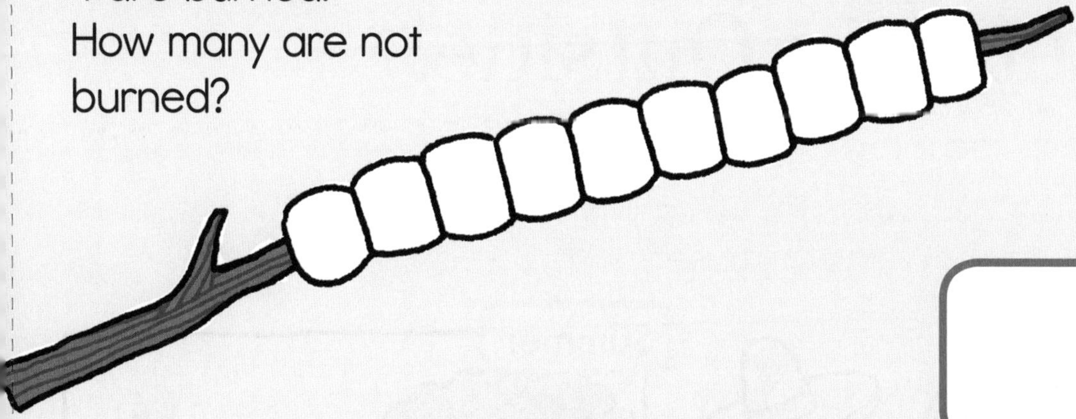

6 are burned.
How many are not burned?

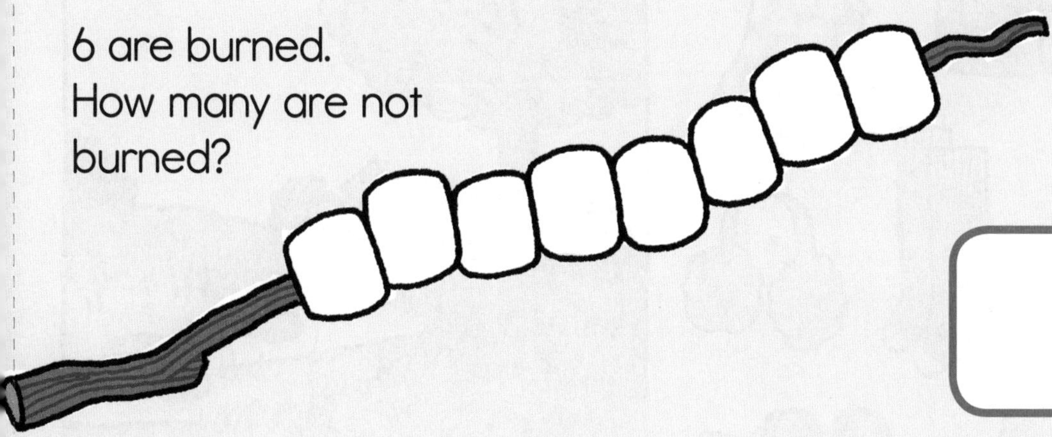

2 are burned.
How many are not burned?

Subtraction

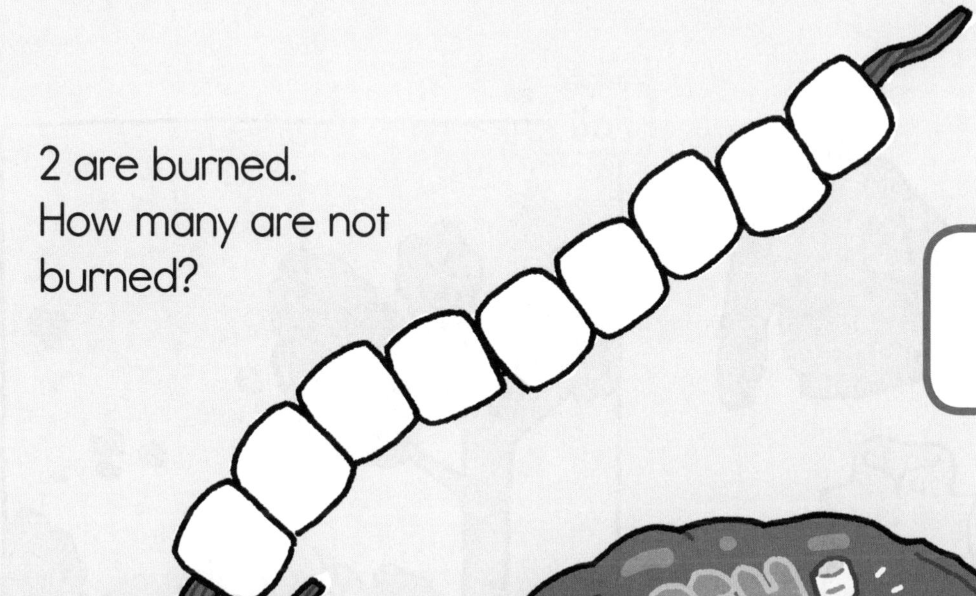

Upon completion, add these stickers to your path on the map!

Four Seasons

Let's Go Outside!

What season is it outside each window? Say the season aloud. Then circle the clothes and gear you might wear and use for that season.

Summer

Fall

Winter

Spring

Upon completion, add these stickers to your path on the map!

BONUS: Which season do plants stop making food and begin shedding their leaves?

Then add this sticker to your map!

Alphabet: R

Rr

Cross out each object that does not begin with **r**.

Write a lowercase **r** to complete each word in each word family.

Upon completion, add this sticker to your path on the map!

sing, thing, __ing

bat, chat, __at

pain, gain, __ain

BONUS: Draw a picture about the characters in the poem.

The rabbit raced the rat around
a racetrack in the rainy town.
They ran and raced,
   to prove who's best,
then the rat and rabbit
   stopped to rest.

Then add this sticker to your map!

Picnic Pests

Ants stole some snacks! Write the equation to find out how many snacks are left.

Subtraction

☐ − ☐ = ☐

☐ − ☐ = ☐

☐ − ☐ = ☐

Upon completion, add this sticker to your path on the map!

Then add this sticker to your map!

BONUS: You have 9 strawberries. Ants carry away 9 strawberries. How many strawberries are left?

☐

All About My Family!

Write and draw about your family.

a picture of my family

A FOOD WE ALL LIKE TO EAT

HOW WE CELEBRATE BIRTHDAYS

Family

a book we like to read

WHAT WE LIKE TO DO OUTSIDE

Upon completion, add these stickers to your path on the map!

BONUS: Draw what your family would bring on an outdoor adventure.

Then add this sticker to your map!

where we live

Alphabet: S

Upon completion, add this sticker to your path on the map!

S s

Color each object that begins with **s**.

Write an uppercase **S** to complete each word.

September

_aturday   _unday

Add a lowercase **s** to make each noun plural. Then read each noun aloud.

star_

shoe_

T t

Circle each object that begins with **t**.

Draw a picture about the poem.

Tie down the tent,
Tend the campfire flames.
Take a trail through the trees,
It's time to play games!

Write the letter **t** to complete each word in each word family.

cop, stop, __op

bent, dent, __ent

boy, joy, __oy

Upon completion, add this sticker to your path on the map!

Classify and
Sort

Where Is It?

Circle the word or
phrase that tells where
each shape is located.

The hexagon is
above below
the tree.

The rectangle is
in front of in back of
the tree.

The circle is
on under
the blanket.

The triangle is **below** **above** the teepee.

The cube is **outside** **inside** the tent.

The cylinder is **next to** **behind** the campfire.

Upon completion, add these stickers to your path on the map!

U u

Circle all of the campers with umbrellas.

Alphabet: U

Fill in each missing **u** to complete each **long u** word.

bl_e

fr_it

j_ice

The word **bug** has a **short u** sound. Circle each object that also has a **short u** sound.

Level 6 complete!

Add this achievement sticker
to your path...

...and move on to

Level 7!

Rules

Following the Rules

Circle the children who are following the rules.

Upon completion, add this sticker to your path on the map!

Brain Box

Rules keep us safe and protect those around us. They also keep our neighborhood and planet clean.

BONUS: Draw a picture of what you wear to stay safe when you ride a bike.

Then add this sticker to your map!

V v

Color each leaf on the vine with **V** or **v**.

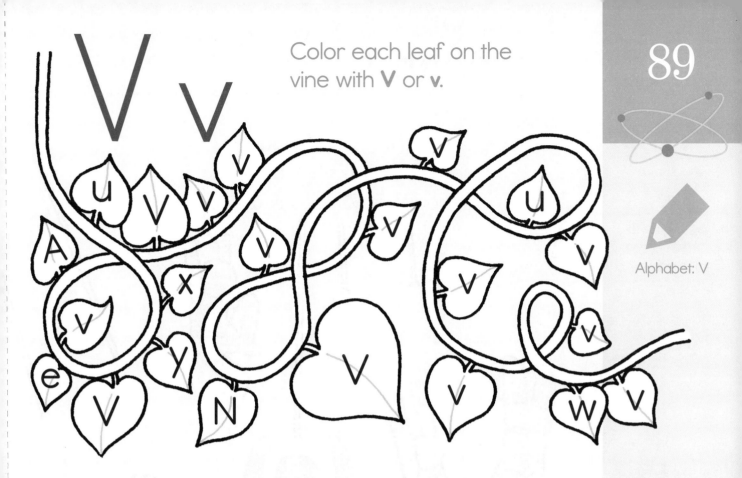

Write a lowercase **v** to complete each noun.

__ase

__an

__egetable

Add an **s** to make each noun plural.
Then read each noun aloud.

violin__

vest__

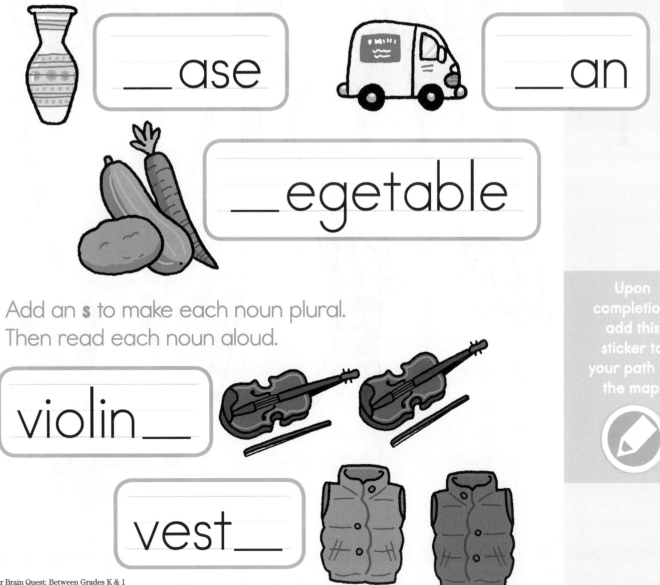

Classify and
Sort

Upon
completion,
add this
sticker to
your path on
the map!

Acrobats!

Look at the number of sides of each trapeze.
Trace the shapes with **3** sides **purple**.
Trace the shapes with **4** sides **blue**.
Trace the shapes with **6** sides **red**.

Count and write the number
of each shape.

_____   _____   _____

Every Animal Is Unique

Read about each animal. Then circle each animal's special body part.

The **anteater** has a long tongue to catch ants.

The **elephant** has tusks to dig water holes.

The **bush pig** has a strong, flat nose to dig up roots to eat.

Brain Box

Animals use their unique features to meet their needs. An anteater's tongue can be up to 2 feet long!

Ww

Alphabet: W

Upon completion, add this sticker to your path on the map!

Color each object that begins with **w**.

Draw a picture about the poem.

Which way did the walrus go?

Why, the weary whale should know.

But when you wish the whale would say,

he just whispers, "He washed away."

BONUS: Write a lowercase w to complete each word.

Then add this sticker to your map!

wheel

__ish

__o__

__agon

X x

Circle each object that begins with **x**.

Alphabet: X

Upon completion, add this sticker to your path on the map!

Write a lowercase **x** to complete each noun.

a__

__-ray

bo__

fo__

Trace the sentence. Capitalize the first letter of the first word of the sentence.

Look at the exciting x-ray!

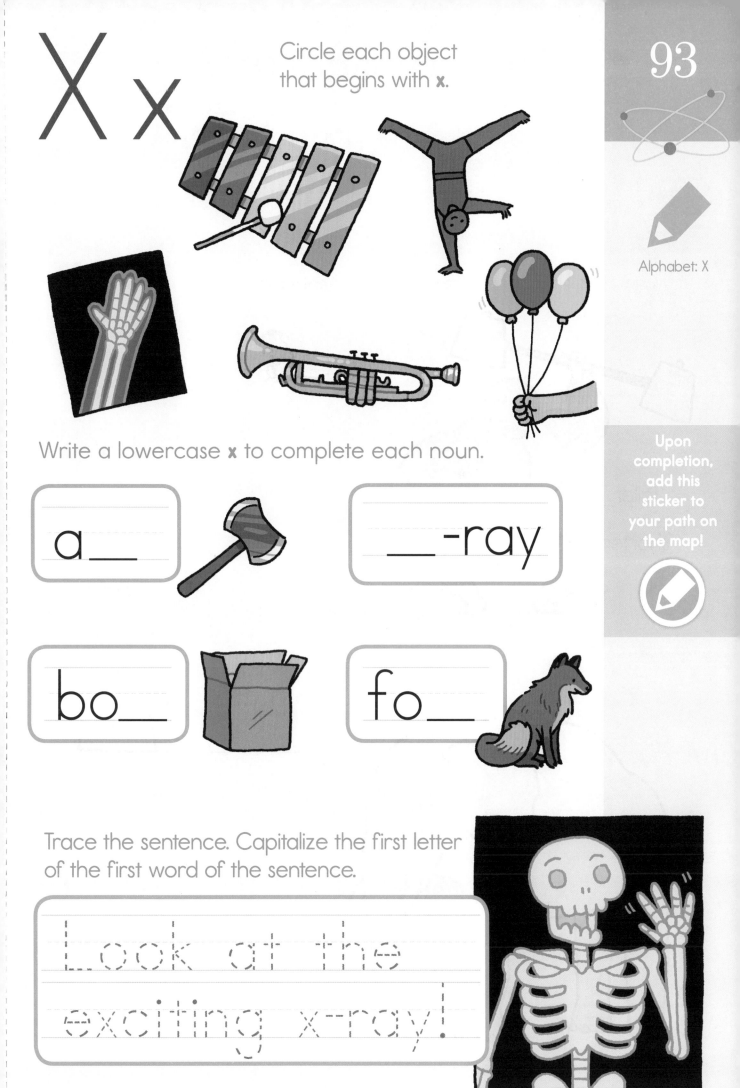

Taller or Shorter?

Are you **taller** or **shorter** than each person, animal, or object? Draw yourself next to it. Then circle taller or shorter.

Measurement

taller

shorter

_____

taller

shorter

_____

taller

shorter

1kg

_____

taller

shorter

_____

Measurement

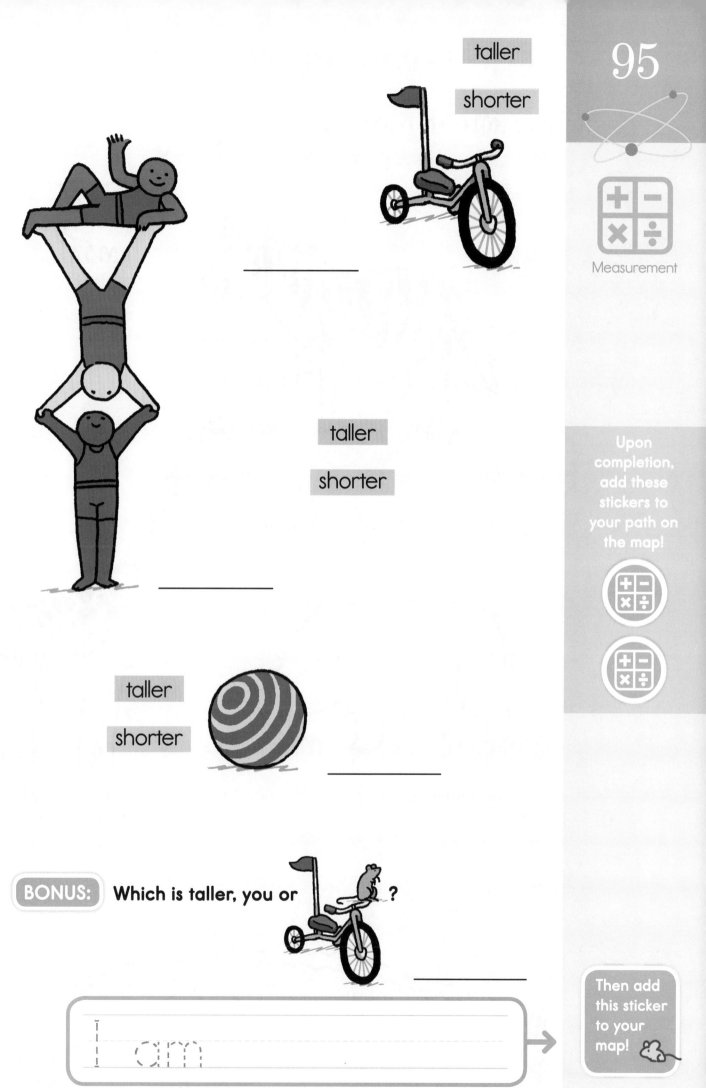

taller
shorter
_____

taller
shorter
_____

taller
shorter
_____

Upon completion, add these stickers to your path on the map!

BONUS: Which is taller, you or _____ ?

I am _____

Then add this sticker to your map!

The Grasslands

Color the animals
and plants that live
in the grasslands.

Zebra

Giraffe

Rhinoceros

Crocodile

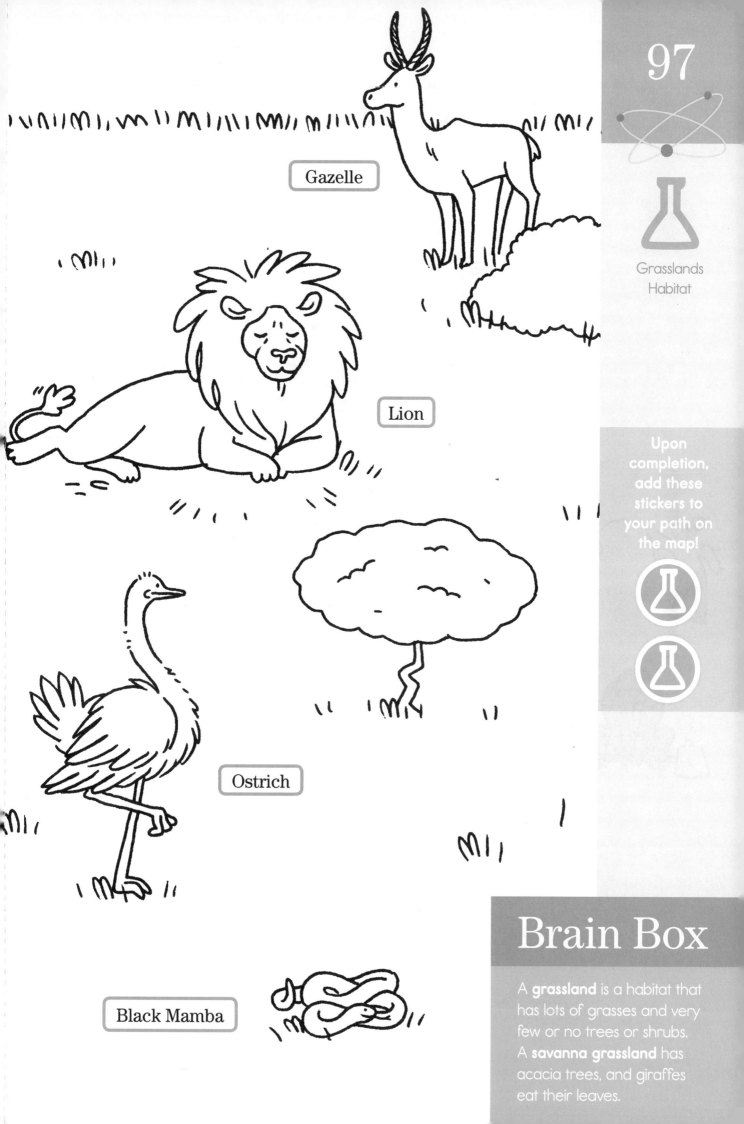

Gazelle

Grasslands
Habitat

Lion

Upon
completion,
add these
stickers to
your path on
the map!

Ostrich

Black Mamba

Brain Box

A **grassland** is a habitat that
has lots of grasses and very
few or no trees or shrubs.
A **savanna grassland** has
acacia trees, and giraffes
eat their leaves.

Alphabet: Y

Yy

Circle each lowercase **y**.

Write a lowercase **y** to complete each verb.

pla__

__ell

tr__

bu__

Trace the sentence. Capitalize the first letter of the first word of each sentence.

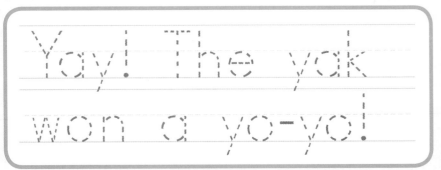

Yay! The yak
won a yo-yo!

Help Is Here!

Draw a picture of each person doing his or her job.

Community Helpers

Forest Worker

Teacher

Construction Worker

Upon completion, add this sticker to your path on the map!

Brain Box

Community helpers provide services that help people. A **service** is an action that meets someone's wants or needs.

Carnival Time!

What time is it? Read each clock and write the time of each event.

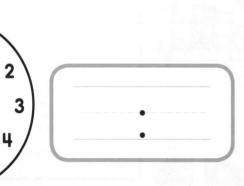

9:00

Time

Upon completion, add these stickers to your path on the map!

Alphabet: Z

Zz

Circle each of the zebra's zucchinis.

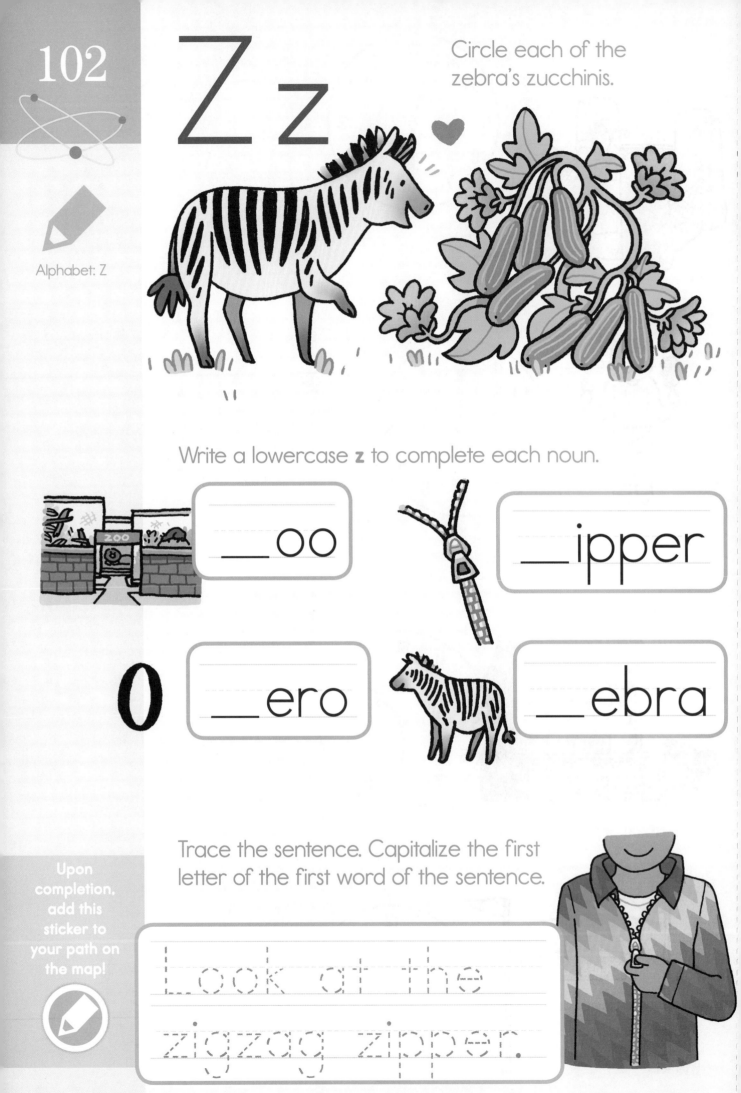

Write a lowercase **z** to complete each noun.

__oo

__ipper

0

__ero

__ebra

Trace the sentence. Capitalize the first letter of the first word of the sentence.

Look at the zigzag zipper.

Upon completion, add this sticker to your path on the map!

Missing Pets

Say the name of the first and second picture aloud.
Then think of a rhyming pet and draw it in its home.

Rhyming

BONUS: Say the name of each picture. Next, draw the person who is missing from the circus tent.

Then add this sticker to your map!

Dizzy Dimes

Count the dimes by tens to get to 100 cents.

10¢

20¢

¢

¢

¢

¢

¢

¢

¢

¢

Upon completion, add this sticker to your path on the map!

Brain Box

A **dime** is **10** cents.

You can write 10 cents like this: **10¢**.

100¢

Level 7 complete!

Add this achievement sticker
to your path…

…and move on to

Level

8!

Snow Train

Fill in the missing question words below.

_____ is the train going?

Where or **Who**

_____ is driving the train?

Who or **When**

_____ is on his head?

Why or **What**

_____ is there a snow plow on the train?

What or **Why**

_____ will the train reach the station?

When or **Who**

Seal Savings!

Count each seal's pennies and dimes and write the amount of money in the box. Then circle the seal that saved the most.

Money

_____ ¢

_____ ¢

_____ ¢

Brain Box

We use **money** to pay people for goods and work. **Pennies** and **dimes** are money.

A penny is worth 1 cent or **1¢**.

A dime is worth 10 cents or **10¢**. Ten pennies make up one dime.

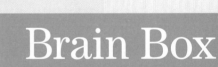

Polar Habitat

Polar Pals

Color the animals and their polar habitat.

Snowy Owl

Fox

Penguin

Moose

Caribou

Upon completion, add this sticker to your path on the map!

Walrus

BONUS: Polar regions are very cold. Seals live in polar regions and have a thick layer of blubber to keep warm. Draw a seal.

Then add this sticker to your map!

Sea Otter

Polar Bear

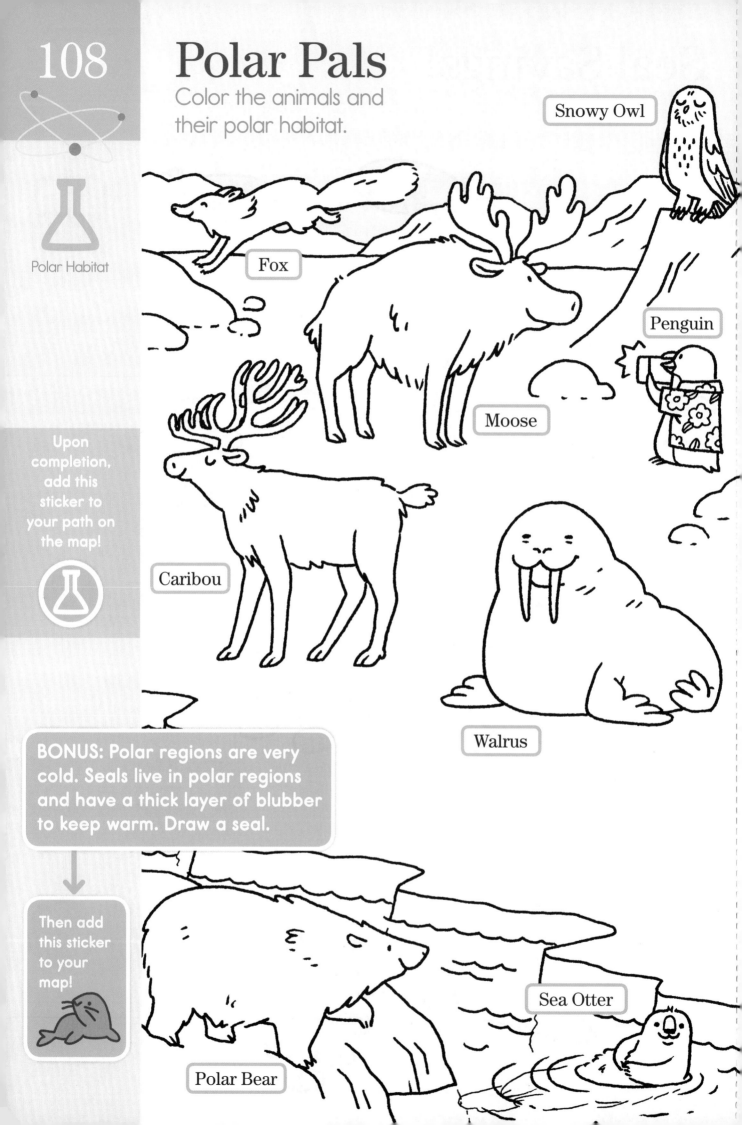

Make Your Own City

Make your own city by drawing man-made structures in this natural environment.

Natural and Man-Made Resources

Upon completion, add this sticker to your path on the map!

Brain Box

Communities have both **natural** and **man-made resources**. Man-made structures include supermarkets, banks, bridges, homes, park benches, and more.

Snowball Snacks

Read the instructions. Draw each step to show how to make a snowball sandwich.

Informational Text

First, get your ingredients: ice cream, 2 cookies, and sprinkles.

Next, scoop ice cream on top of 1 cookie.

Next, put the other cookie on top to make a sandwich.

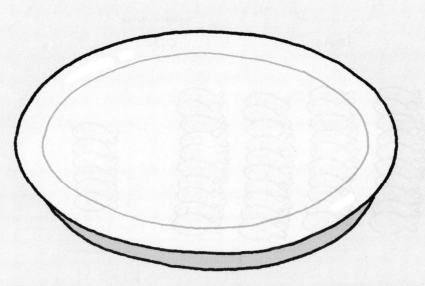

Last, add sprinkles around the edge and enjoy!

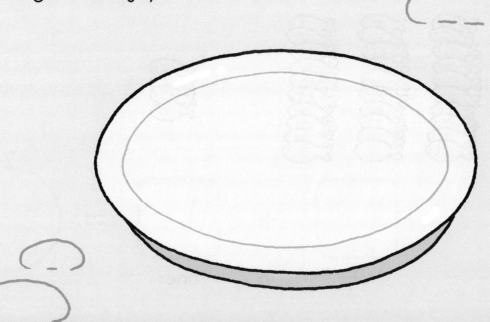

Upon completion, add these stickers to your path on the map!

Counting Fish

Count each group of fish. Write
each number in the box below.
Then write the total in the circle.

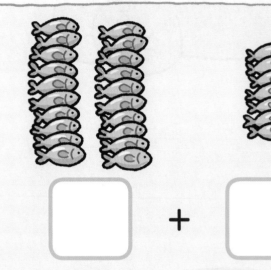

☐ **tens** + ☐ **ones** = ◯

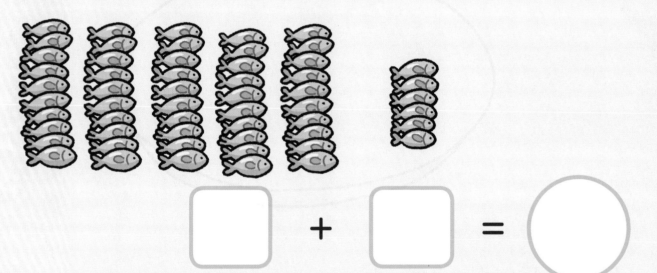

☐ **tens** + ☐ **ones** = ◯

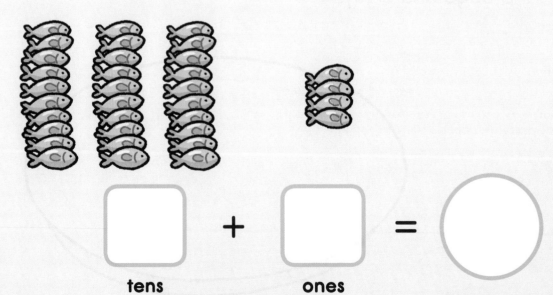

☐ **tens** + ☐ **ones** = ◯

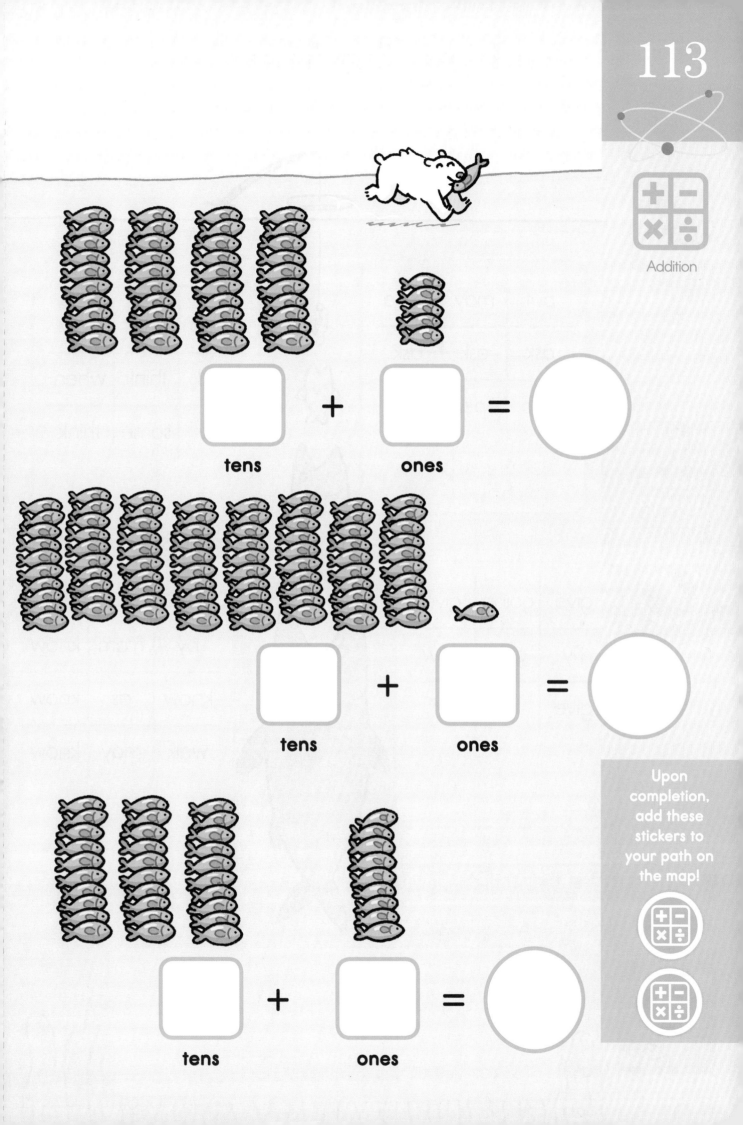

Addition

☐ + ☐ = ◯
tens   ones

☐ + ☐ = ◯
tens   ones

☐ + ☐ = ◯
tens   ones

Upon completion, add these stickers to your path on the map!

Fishing for Matches

In each tic-tac-toe board, draw a line through the matching words. Then write the matching word below.

Sight Words

Upon completion, add this sticker to your path on the map!

put	may	were
ask	ask	ask
stop	open	just

ask

think	after	how
old	think	when
live	some	think

give	going	give
fly	give	how
give	let	of

by	from	know
know	as	know
walk	may	know

BONUS: Trace the sentence below:

Then add this sticker to your map!

Which fish will eat the worm?

100 Ice Cubes!

Fill in the missing numbers to count to 100.
Start at 1 and write the numbers in order.

Counting

Upon completion, add this sticker to your path on the map!

1	2			5	6	7		9	
	12	13	14				18	19	20
21			24	25		27	28		
		33	34	35	36			39	
	42	43			46	47	48	49	
51	52	53		55			58		60
61			64	65		67		69	
	72	73	74		76		78	79	
81					86	87		89	
		93	94	95					100

Let's Get Moving!

Circle the person who is **pushing**.
Then draw something in the sled!

Push and Pull

Upon completion, add this sticker to your path on the map!

Circle the person who is **pulling**.
Then draw something in the sled!

Brain Box

Pushing an object moves it away from you. **Pulling** an object moves it closer to you.

Punctuation with Penguins

Draw a line to match each punctuation mark with its name.

Punctuation

Upon completion, add this sticker to your path on the map!

Fill in the correct punctuation mark at the end of each sentence.

Penguins have wings but cannot fly ____

Can a penguin swim ____

Penguins are amazing animals ____

More Penguins

Count the penguins on each ice island. Write the numbers in the boxes. Then write the sum.

[ ] + [ ] = [ ]

[ ] + [ ] = [ ]

Addition

[ ] + [ ] = [ ]

Upon completion, add these stickers to your path on the map!

[ ] + [ ] = [ ]

BONUS: If 5 icebergs + 5 icebergs equals 10 icebergs, what is 5 icebergs + 6 icebergs?

[____ icebergs]

Then add this sticker to your map!

Playing with Shadows

Draw what animal each shadow looks like to you!

Shadows

Brain Box

A **shadow** is a dark shape caused when someone or something blocks a source of light. A shadow can be cast from the sun, a light in your house, or even a flashlight.

Shadows

Upon completion, add these stickers to your path on the map!

CONGRATULATIONS!
You completed all of your science quests! You earned:

Hungry Harp Seal

Circle the correct **adjective** to complete each sentence. Then draw a picture about the story.

Upon completion, add this sticker to your path on the map!

This **hungry** **sleepy** harp seal pup wants a snack. To get food, he dives under the **blue** **yellow** water. He hunts for **fresh** **old** fish. When he swims to catch them, he is **fast** **slow** !

Animal Tracks!

Write each sum. Then answer the question.

3 + 4 =

4 + 3 =

Upon completion, add this sticker to your path on the map!

4 + 6 =

6 + 4 =

Can you add in any order? Answer **yes** or **no**.

CONGRATULATIONS!
You completed all of your math quests! You earned:

To the Igloo!

Read the directions. Then draw a line to lead the penguin to the igloo.

N
W E
S

Move 3 spaces north.

Move 2 spaces east.

Move 1 space north.

Move 4 spaces east.

Move 1 space north.

Maps and Directions

Upon completion, add these stickers to your path on the map!

CONGRATULATIONS! You completed all of your social studies quests! You earned:

Poetry

What Will You Discover?

Read the poem about the author's favorite book. Then write a poem or draw a picture about your favorite book.

I open the cover
and turn the pages.
I'm on a plane!
I'm on a train!
I see grassland.
A beach of sand.
The Arctic ice.
The ocean, twice!
I can drive a car
to travel far.
What will you discover
behind your book cover?

Upon completion, add this sticker to your path on the map!

CONGRATULATIONS!
You completed all of your English language arts quests! You earned:

Quest complete!

Add this achievement sticker to your path...

QUEST complete! Welcome to 1st grade!

...and turn to the next page for your Summer Brainiac Award!

Summer Brainiac Award!

You have completed your entire Summer Brain Quest! Woo-hoo! Congratulations! That's quite an achievement.

Write your name on the line and cut out the award certificate. Show your friends. Hang it on your wall! You're a certified Summer Brainiac!

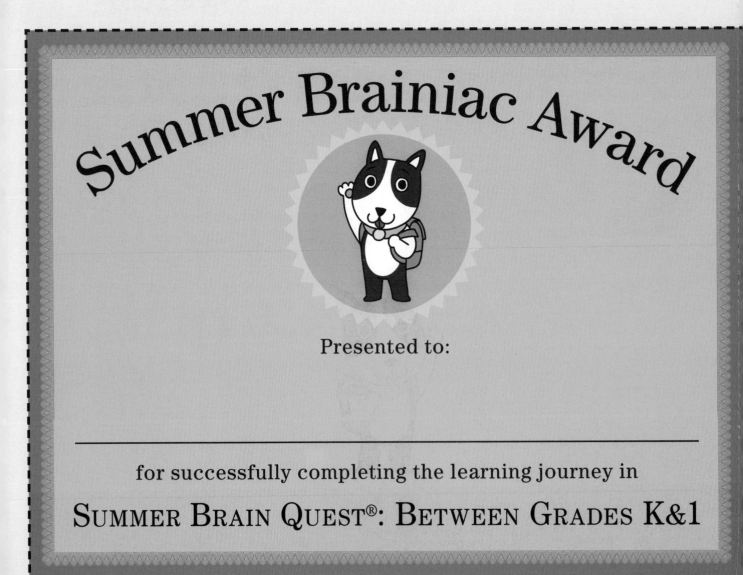

Summer Brainiac Award

Presented to:

_____

for successfully completing the learning journey in

SUMMER BRAIN QUEST®: BETWEEN GRADES K&1

Outside Quests

This is not just a workbook—it's a scavenger hunt, a game of opposites, a way to enjoy the summer sunshine, and so much more! Summer is the perfect time to explore the great outdoors. Use the Outside Quests to make your next sunny day more fun than ever—and earn an achievement sticker.

Outside
Quests

Then add this sticker to your map!

Level 1

Letter Hunt

What is the first letter of your name? Find an object in nature that starts with the same letter. Next, find an object for each of the remaining letters in your name. Play again with the name of a friend or family member.

Level 2

Helpers and Heroes

Who are the community helpers in your neighborhood? Go for a walk. Point to the ways in which they help your community. For example, you can point to a recycling bin and talk about recycling collectors.

Then add this sticker to your map!

◈ Level 3 Shadow Tag

Find a partner. Pick someone to be "it" and start running around, looking for your shadows. When whoever is "it" steps on the other person's shadow, that person then becomes "it." Play at different times of the day to see how your shadows change!

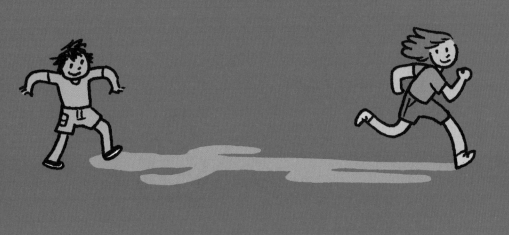

Then add this sticker to your map!

◈ Level 3 Shape Search

Go to a park. Look for triangles, squares, and circles around you. Point to and name each shape.

Then add this sticker to your map!

Outside
Quests

Then add this sticker to your map!

✦ Level 5 ✦ Outdoor Opposites

Find a partner. Make a movement and then have your partner do the opposite. For example, you can jump high and your partner can crouch low in the grass. Now it's your partner's turn to make a movement and your turn to do the opposite.

✦ Level 6 ✦ Scavenger Hunt

Find a partner. Ask your partner to close his or her eyes while you hide an object such as a ball or rock. Now it's time for your partner to search for it! Give your partner clues about how to find the object by using words like these: up, down, over, under, left, right, or behind. Once your partner finds the object, it's his or her turn to hide an object and your turn to search!

Then add this sticker to your map!

Counting Critters

Level 7

Go for a walk and look for groups of animals! Compare the numbers of animals that you see. For example, do you see 2 dogs? Do you see 5 birds? Are there more or fewer birds than dogs?

Then add this sticker to your map!

Animal Home Detective

Level 8

Search for animal homes. Look for holes and burrows in the ground or nests and hives in trees, or anywhere else animals might be living. Remember not to touch! What animals live in these homes? Why? Get a sheet of paper, and draw the animals in their homes.

Then add this sticker to your map!

Answer Key

(For pages or answers not included
in this section, answers will vary.)

Ready for Takeoff!
Read the alphabet aloud, and fill in the missing uppercase letters.

Desert Digits
Trace the numbers in the sand. Then circle your age.

Train Travel
Read the train's directions. Then draw a line on the tracks to help the train find the treasure.

Go UP to the cactus.
Travel BEHIND the mountains.
Make a RIGHT before the sand castle.
End your trip BETWEEN the shovels!

START
END

Dressing for the Desert
The camel is going on a trip through the hot, dry desert. Say the word for each picture, and cross out the items he will NOT need to pack for this weather.

BONUS: Write or draw a picture of what you wear when the weather is hot.

13

Welcome Home!
The Gila woodpecker lives in a desert cactus. Write or draw about what happens when he gets to his home. What might he find there? What might he do there?

BONUS: Write the word "cactus."

cactus

Hide-and-Seek
Count the number of each animal. Then write the number.

6 hawks
2 rams
8 owls
9 butterflies
3 deer
1 tortoise
5 rabbits
4 toads
7 geckos

BONUS: Find the sticks that form a number. What number is it?
4
How many sticks form the number?
4

Search for Shadows
The sun is shining, and it's hot in the desert. Animals need shade and water to survive. Draw a line to help the camel to the cool oasis.

A a
Color each apple with A or a.

Write an uppercase A to complete each word.

April   August   America

The word hot has a short a sound. Circle each object that also has a short a sound.

Let's Get Digging!
Draw a line to match each community helper with his or her tools.

Lifeguard
Police Officer
Sanitation Worker
Emergency Medical Responder

Treasure Hunt!
Count the number of each type of treasure. Then write the number.

11
18
19
12
14
14 18 13 17

BONUS: Draw your own gems. Then write the number of gems you draw.

Coyote Chase
Look at each picture. What happens first, second, third, and last? Draw a line to match each event to the correct order on the timeline.

FIRST
LAST

BONUS: What could happen next? Draw an ending in the box at the end of the timeline.

Bb

Color each object that begins with **b**.

Draw a picture about the poem.

I see a busy bumblebee,
bronze and black.
He's buzzing by the beehive,
wings buzzing on his back.

Write a lowercase **b** to complete each word.

baby   **b**read

bear   **b**ird

Cc

Circle the crabs and clams.

Write a lowercase **c** to complete each word in each word family.

rat, bat, **c**at

now, plow, **c**ow

map, snap, **c**ap

Trace the sentence. Capitalize the first letter of the first word of the sentence.

I see a colorful clam on the coral.

Beach Day!

Find the shapes. Color the circles **yellow**. Color the squares **green**. Color the rectangles **blue**. Color the triangles **red**.

BONUS: Draw a shape. Then color it to look like something you might find at a beach.

Dd

Circle each animal that begins with **d**.

Draw a picture about the poem.

The dizzy dizzy dump truck dumped his load of dirt.
It landed on the driver, but at least he wasn't hurt!

Write a lowercase **d** to complete each word.

day   **d**og

did   **d**ad

Ee

Circle each segment with lowercase **e**.

The word **net** has a **short e** sound. Circle each object that also has a **short e** sound.

Fill in each missing **e** to complete each **long e** word.

b**ee**   l**ea**f

tr**ee**

Game On!

Draw a line to match each shape with its name.

sphere

cylinder

cube

cone

BONUS: What solid and flat shapes can you find at a baseball park? Write or draw the shapes.

Then add this sticker to your path!

Make a Match

Draw on the right what is missing from each animal home on the left.

Ff

Circle each food that begins with **f**.

Write a lowercase **f** to complete each verb.

fall   **f**ind

fly   **f**ix

Add an **s** to make each noun plural. Then read each word aloud.

football**s**   flower**s**

Gg

Color all of the golf balls, golf carts, and gophers.

Write a lowercase **g** to complete each word in each word family.

boat, coat, **g**oat

drum, hum, **g**um

date, late, **g**ate

Add an **s** to make each noun plural. Then read each word aloud.

girl**s**   game**s**

Anthill Map

Read the map key. Color each entrance **green**. Color each nursery **red**. Color each food storage room **orange**. Color the queen's room **yellow**. Color the rest area **blue**.

Map Key
Entrance
Nursery
Food Storage Room
Queen's Room
Rest Area

Flat or Solid

Color all the shapes. Then draw a circle around the flat shapes and a square around the solid shapes.

sphere

circle

cone

rectangle

square

cube

triangle

cylinder

ICE CREAM

ORDER HERE

Hh

Circle each object that begins with **h**.

Trace the sentence. Capitalize the first letter of the first word of the sentence.

Look at the hair on
the horses' heads.

Write a lowercase **h** to complete each verb.

hold

hurt

help

Ii

Circle each lowercase letter **i**.

Fill in each missing **i** to complete each **long i** word. Then read the sentence aloud.

I like to ride my bike.

The word **mitt** has a **short i** sound. Circle each object that also has a **short i** sound. Then read the word aloud.

Goal!

Draw 10 soccer balls in the left net. Then draw the missing balls in the right net to match the total. Next trace the equation.

10 + 1 = 11

10 + 7 = 17

10 + 5 = 15

10 + 9 = 19

10 + 3 = 13

Let's Go Shopping!

Match each item on the shopping list to the store where you can buy it.

Shopping List
Books
Ballet Slippers
Bananas
Hammer
Flowers

BONUS: Draw a place where you can buy ice cream next to the grocery store. It can be a store, a stand, or a truck!

Then add this sticker to your map!

Draw Your Own Plant

A plant has parts that help it grow. Draw your own plant and label the parts.

flower

leaf

stem

roots

flower

leaf

stem

roots

seeds

BONUS: Plants grow from seeds. Draw some seeds in the soil above to grow more plants!

Then add this sticker to your map!

More Animals!

Count the animals in each group and write the number. Then circle which group has more.

2

3

BONUS

3

6

4

5

BONUS: Circle the group that has the most animals.

Then add this sticker to your map!

Natural Resources

Draw and color living natural resources to complete the farm.

Answers
may vary.

Brain Box

Natural resources are all of the living and nonliving things in nature that we use to help us live. Plants and animals are examples of **living resources**. Dirt, rocks, and water are examples of **nonliving resources.**

BONUS: Draw a farmer using a nonliving and a living natural resource.

Then add this sticker to your map!

Jj

Color all of the jaguar's jars of jelly.

Write an uppercase **J** to complete each word.

January

June

July

Write a lowercase **j** to complete each verb. Then read each verb aloud.

jump

jog

Kk

Color each kite with **K** or **k**.

Write a lowercase **k** to complete each verb.

kick

keep

kiss

Add an **s** to make each noun plural. Then read each word aloud.

kids

kites

Growing Groups

Count each group of vegetables. Then write the sum in the box.

= 5

= 6

= 10

= 7

= 7

= 8

= 6

BONUS: How many and are there in all?

11

Then add this sticker to your map!

Ll

Color each object that begins with **l**.

Draw a picture about the poem.

The lost lightning bug leaped
and landed in the lake tonight.
It's dark beneath the water
but he won't turn on his light.

lake
ladder
logs

BONUS: Look at the picture and write each word that begins with "l."

Then add this sticker to your map!

Mm

Circle each object that begins with **m**.

Write an uppercase **M** to complete each word.

| March | May | Monday |

Write a lowercase **m** to complete each word.

| man | mat |
| mud | mom |

Flower Power

Draw flowers to show the total, then write the total in the box.

7

2 + 6   8

9

Let's Get Growing!

The seeds in the soil have the water and sunlight they need to grow. Draw what they will grow into!

PUMPKIN   SUNFLOWER   APPLE TREE

BONUS: These plants get water from a watering can. Draw another way that plants can get water above.

Then add this sticker to your map!

Time for School!

Draw a line to help the girl through her morning routine on her way to school. Describe each step aloud.

Brain Quest Elementary School

Nn

Color each nut with an uppercase **N**.

Trace the sentence. Capitalize the first letter of the first word of the sentence.

There are nine newts in the net.

Write a lowercase **n** to complete each word.

night   nail   nest

Oo

Circle each owl egg with **O** or **o**.

The word **moth** has a **short o** sound. Circle each object that also has a **short o** sound.

Fill in each missing **o** to complete each **short** and **long o** word. Then read the sentences aloud.

Oh no! The dog lost his bone.

Fly Your Flag!

Color the American flag.

Next, draw a flag to represent your family!

Brain Box

July 4th is **Independence Day**. In 1776, the 13 original colonies declared themselves a new nation, the United States of America. The American flag is the national flag of the United States of America. There are 13 stripes (one for each original colony) and 50 stars (one for each state).

Pp

Color each object that begins with **p**.

Write a lowercase **p** to complete each word.

| pig | pop |
| pat | pup |

Draw a picture about the poem.

The pretty pig and pink piglet paddled past the park. What a peaceful plan they picked, until they saw a shark!

Night Animals!

Count the animals in each group. Write the numbers and the total.

1 + 4 = 5

7 + 2 = 9

4 + 3 = 7

3 + 3 = 6

2 + 3 = 5

BONUS: Draw one more raccoon in the group above. Now how many raccoons are there in all? 6

Then add this sticker to your map!

Animals of the Meadow

Draw the missing animals to make a group of 10. Then write the numbers that add to 10.

9 + 1 = 10

5 + 5 = 10

7 + 3 = 10

Qq

Write **quack** for each quacking duck.

quack   quack   quack

Write a lowercase **q** to complete each noun.

| quail | question |
| quilt | quarter |

Add an **s** to make each noun plural. Then read each noun aloud.

quarts

queens

74

Marshmallow Math

Count the marshmallows. Color the number that are burned in black. Write the number of marshmallows that are not burned.

3 are burned. How many are not burned?   2

4 are burned. How many are not burned?   4

2 are burned. How many are not burned?   5

4 are burned. How many are not burned?   6

6 are burned. How many are not burned?   2

2 are burned. How many are not burned?   7

Let's Go Outside!

What season is it outside each window? Say the season aloud. Then circle the clothes and gear you might wear and use for that season.

Summer

Winter

Spring

Fall

77

BONUS: Which season do plants stop making food and begin shedding their leaves?

Fall

Then add this sticker to your map!

Rr

Cross out each object that does not begin with r.

Write a lowercase r to complete each word in each word family.

sing, thing, _r_ing

bat, chat, _r_at

pain, gain, _r_ain

BONUS: Draw a picture about the characters in the poem.

The rabbit raced the rat around
a racetrack in the rainy town.
They ran and raced,
to prove who's best,
then the rat and rabbit
stopped to rest.

Then add this sticker to your map!

Picnic Pests

Ants stole some snacks! Write the equation to find out how many snacks are left.

$$8 - 2 = 6$$

$$7 - 2 = 5$$

$$4 - 3 = 1$$

BONUS: You have 4 strawberries. Ants carry away 4 strawberries. How many strawberries are left?

0

S s

Color each object that begins with s.

Write an uppercase S to complete each word.

September

_S_aturday   _S_unday

Add a lowercase s to make each noun plural. Then read each noun aloud.

star_s_

shoe_s_

T t

Circle each object that begins with t.

Draw a picture about the poem.

Tie down the tent.
Tend the campfire flames.
Take a trail through the trees,
It's time to play games!

Write the letter t to complete each word in each word family.

cop, stop, _t_op

bent, dent, _t_ent

boy, joy, _t_oy

Where Is It?

Circle the word or phrase that tells where each shape is located.

The triangle is (below) above the teepee.

The hexagon is (above) below the tree.

The cube is outside (inside) the tent.

The rectangle is (in front of) in back of the tree.

The cylinder is (next to) behind the campfire.

The circle is (on) under the blanket.

U u

Circle all of the campers with umbrellas.

Fill in each missing u to complete each long u word.

bl_u_e

fr_u_it

j_u_ice

The word bug has a short u sound. Circle each object that also has a short u sound.

Following the Rules

Circle the children who are following the rules.

Brain Box

Rules keep us safe and protect those around us. They also keep our neighborhoods and homes clean.

BONUS: Draw a picture of what you wear to stay safe when you ride a bike.

Then add this sticker to your map!

V v

Color each leaf on the vine with V or v.

Write a lowercase v to complete each noun.

_v_ase

_v_an

_v_egetable

Add an s to make each noun plural. Then read each noun aloud.

violin_s_

vest_s_

Acrobats!

Look at the number of sides of each trapeze.
Trace the shapes with 3 sides purple.
Trace the shapes with 4 sides blue.
Trace the shapes with 6 sides red.

Count and write the number of each shape.

△ 3   ☐ 4   ⬡ 2

Every Animal Is Unique

Read about each animal. Then circle each animal's special body part.

The anteater has a long tongue to catch ants.

The elephant has tusks to dig water holes.

The bush pig has a strong, flat nose to dig up roots to eat.

Brain Box

W w

Color each object that begins with w.

Draw a picture about the poem.

Which way did the walrus go?
Why, the weary whale should know.
But when you wish the whale would say,
he just whispers, "He washed away."

BONUS: Write a lowercase w to complete each word.

wheel   wish

wow   wagon

X x

Circle each object that begins with x.

Write a lowercase x to complete each noun.

a_x_   _x_-ray

bo_x_   fo_x_

Trace the sentence. Capitalize the first letter of the first word of the sentence.

Look at the exciting x-ray!

Taller or Shorter?

Are you **taller** or **shorter** than each person, animal, or object? Draw yourself next to it. Then circle taller or shorter.

taller / shorter (multiple instances)

BONUS: Which is taller, you or ?

I am taller.

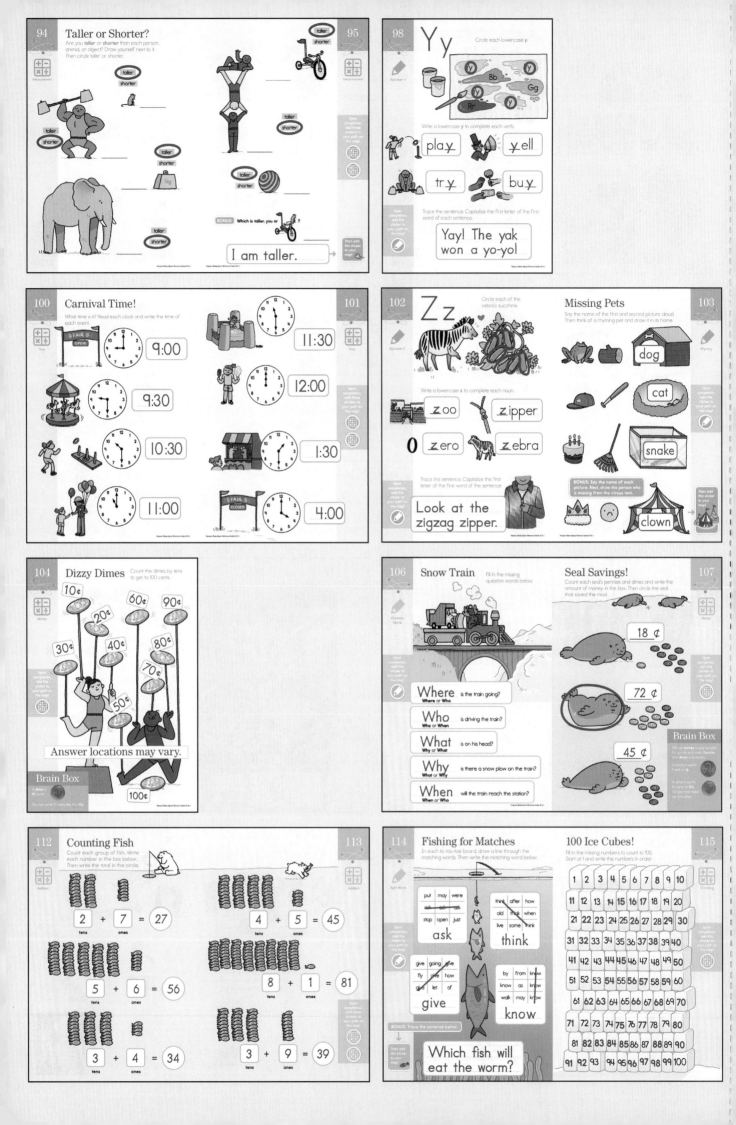

Y y

Circle each lowercase y.

Write a lowercase **y** to complete each verb.

pla**y**   **y**ell
tr**y**   bu**y**

Trace the sentence. Capitalize the first letter of the first word of each sentence.

Yay! The yak won a yo-yo!

Carnival Time!

What time is it? Read each clock and write the time of each event.

9:00   11:30
9:30   12:00
10:30   1:30
11:00   4:00

Z z

Circle each of the zebra's zucchinis.

Write a lowercase **z** to complete each noun.

zoo   **z**ipper
zero   **z**ebra

Trace the sentence. Capitalize the first letter of the first word of the sentence.

Look at the zigzag zipper.

Missing Pets

Say the name of the first and second picture aloud. Then think of a rhyming pet and draw it in its home.

dog
cat
snake

BONUS: Say the name of each picture. Next, draw the person who is missing from the circus tent.

clown

Dizzy Dimes

Count the dimes by tens to get to 100 cents.

10¢ 20¢ 30¢ 40¢ 50¢ 60¢ 70¢ 80¢ 90¢ 100¢

Answer locations may vary.

Brain Box

A **dime** is worth 10 cents.

You can write 10 cents like this: 10¢.

Snow Train

Fill in the missing question words below.

Where is the train going?
Where or Who

Who is driving the train?
Who or When

What is on his head?
Why or What

Why is there a snow plow on the train?
What or Why

When will the train reach the station?
When or Who

Seal Savings!

Count each seal's pennies and dimes and write the amount of money in the box. Then circle the seal that saved the most.

18 ¢
72 ¢
45 ¢

Brain Box

We use **money** to pay people for goods and work. Pennies and dimes are money.

A penny is worth 1 cent or 1¢.

A dime is worth 10 cents or 10¢. Ten pennies make one dime.

Counting Fish

Count each group of fish. Write each number in the box below. Then write the total in the circle.

2 + 7 = 27
tens ones

4 + 5 = 45
tens ones

5 + 6 = 56
tens ones

8 + 1 = 81
tens ones

3 + 4 = 34
tens ones

3 + 9 = 39
tens ones

Fishing for Matches

In each tic-tac-toe board, draw a line through the matching words. Then write the matching word below.

put	may	were
ask	ask	ask
stop	open	just

ask

think	after	how
old	think	when
live	some	think

think

give	going	give
fly	give	how
give	let	of

give

by	from	knew
know	as	know
walk	may	know

know

BONUS: Trace the sentence below.

Which fish will eat the worm?

100 Ice Cubes!

Fill in the missing numbers to count to 100. Start at 1 and write the numbers in order.

1	2	3	4	5	6	7	8	9	10
11	12	13	14	15	16	17	18	19	20
21	22	23	24	25	26	27	28	29	30
31	32	33	34	35	36	37	38	39	40
41	42	43	44	45	46	47	48	49	50
51	52	53	54	55	56	57	58	59	60
61	62	63	64	65	66	67	68	69	70
71	72	73	74	75	76	77	78	79	80
81	82	83	84	85	86	87	88	89	90
91	92	93	94	95	96	97	98	99	100

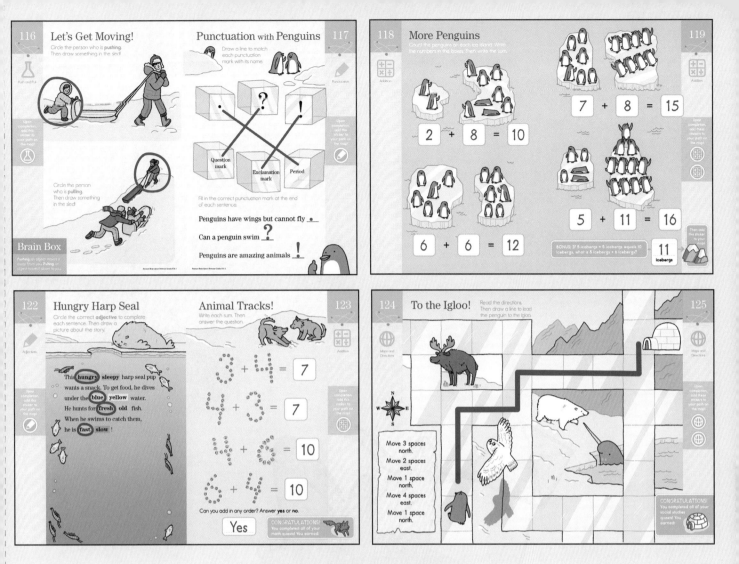

Summer Brain Quest Extras

Stay smart all summer long with these Summer Brain Quest Extras! In this section you'll find:

Summer Brain Quest Reading List

A book can take you anywhere—and summer is a great time to go on a reading adventure! Use the Summer Brain Quest Reading List to help you start the next chapter of your quest!

Summer Brain Quest Mini Deck

Cut out the cards and make your own Summer Brain Quest Mini Deck. Play by yourself or with a friend.

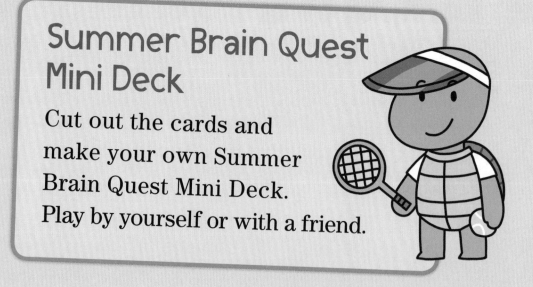

Summer Brain Quest Reading List

We recommend reading at least 15 to 30 minutes each day. Read to yourself or aloud. You can also read aloud with a friend or family member and discuss the book. Here are some questions to get you started:

- Was the book a nonfiction (informational) or fiction (story/narrative) text?
- Who or what was the book about?
- What was the setting of the story (where did it take place)?
- Was there a main character? Who is it? Describe the character.
- Was there a problem in the story? What was it? How was it solved?
- Were there any themes in the story?
- Were there any lessons in the story?
- Why do you think the author wrote the book?

Jump-start your reading adventure by visiting your local library or bookstore and checking out the following books. Track which ones you've read, and write your own review! Would you recommend this book to a friend? Who would you recommend this book to, and why?

Fiction

Amazing Grace, written by Mary Hoffman, illustrated by Caroline Binch

Grace's class is putting on *Peter Pan*. Grace tries out for the lead, but her classmates complain that she doesn't look the part: She's a girl, and she's black. Read how Grace proves them wrong.

DATE STARTED: _____   DATE FINISHED: _____

MY REVIEW: _____

_____

Chicka Chicka Boom Boom, written by Bill Martin, Jr., and John Archambault, illustrated by Lois Ehlert

Race the letters of the alphabet up a coconut tree!

DATE STARTED: _____   DATE FINISHED: _____

MY REVIEW: _____

_____

Corduroy, by Don Freeman

Corduroy is a lonely teddy bear who is stuck on a department store shelf. No one wants to buy him because his overalls are missing a button, so he sets out on a mission to find one.

DATE STARTED: _____   DATE FINISHED: _____

MY REVIEW: _____

_____

Don't Throw It to Mo! written by David A. Adler, illustrated by Sam Ricks

Mo loves playing football, even though he may not be the fastest or the biggest player on the team. His friends don't mind, but their rival team teases him for being so small. Will Mo let their teasing stop him?

DATE STARTED: _____   DATE FINISHED: _____

MY REVIEW: _____

_____

Frog and Toad All Year, by Arnold Lobel

Frog and Toad are best friends, and they stick together through all kinds of adventures. Follow them through the seasons, from sticky summer to fresh fall and white winter, until a springy spring.

DATE STARTED: _____   DATE FINISHED: _____

MY REVIEW: _____

_____

Ira Sleeps Over, by Bernard Waber

Ira is excited to sleep over at his friend Reggie's house for the first time . . . until his sister asks whether he's going to bring his teddy bear along. He's never slept without his teddy bear before. What if Reggie makes fun of him?

DATE STARTED: _____   DATE FINISHED: _____

MY REVIEW: _____

_____

Leo the Late Bloomer, written by Robert Kraus, illustrated by Jose Aruego

Leo's father is worried—Leo isn't reading, writing, drawing, or speaking yet. But Leo's mother knows that Leo is going to do all of these things—and more! But when?

DATE STARTED: _____ DATE FINISHED: _____

MY REVIEW: _____

_____

The Napping House, written by Audrey Wood, illustrated by Don Wood

One rainy afternoon, Granny is snoring on a cozy bed. She is joined by a dreaming child, a dozing dog, and more animal characters until the bed is about to burst!

DATE STARTED: _____ DATE FINISHED: _____

MY REVIEW: _____

_____

This Is Me: A Story of Who We Are and Where We Come From, written by Jamie Lee Curtis, illustrated by Laura Cornell

People immigrate to America from all over the world, sometimes with just one suitcase to call their own. Discover different stories of families that have moved and what they brought to their new home.

DATE STARTED: _____ DATE FINISHED: _____

MY REVIEW: _____

_____

The Very Hungry Caterpillar, by Eric Carle

The snow has finally melted, and this caterpillar has quite the spring-time appetite!

DATE STARTED: _____   DATE FINISHED: _____

MY REVIEW: _____

_____

Where the Wild Things Are, by Maurice Sendak

Max gets into trouble wherever he goes. When he is sent to his bedroom, it becomes a jungle filled with monsters, and Max goes on his greatest adventure of all!

DATE STARTED: _____   DATE FINISHED: _____

MY REVIEW: _____

_____

Whistle for Willie, by Ezra Jack Keats

Peter wants to learn how to whistle for his dog, Willie. But the only people he sees whistling are grown-ups. How will he learn?

DATE STARTED: _____   DATE FINISHED: _____

MY REVIEW: _____

_____

Nonfiction

A Second Is a Hiccup, written by Hazel Hutchins, illustrated by Kady MacDonald Denton

How long is a second? This book makes counting easy—you can count while you jump rope, climb a tree, or even grow into a new pair of shoes!

DATE STARTED: _____   DATE FINISHED: _____

MY REVIEW: _____

_____

Beautiful Oops! written and illustrated by Barney Saltzberg

A spill doesn't ruin a drawing—not when it becomes the shape of a goofy animal. A mistake is just an adventure in creativity!

DATE STARTED: _____   DATE FINISHED: _____

MY REVIEW: _____

_____

Castle: How It Works, by David Macaulay

Go back in time and take a tour of a castle's secret passageways—just watch out for the dungeon!

DATE STARTED: _____   DATE FINISHED: _____

MY REVIEW: _____

_____

For the Love of Soccer! written by Pelé, illustrated by Frank Morrison

Pelé knew he wanted to be a soccer star from a very young age. But it wasn't easy—he had to practice hard, stay in school, and learn to work as a teammate. Read about following your dreams.

DATE STARTED: _____   DATE FINISHED: _____

MY REVIEW: _____

_____

I'm a Caterpillar, written by Jean Marzollo, illustrated by Judith Moffatt

It started off as a tiny egg, then hatched into a caterpillar, and now an even more beautiful shape awaits. . . .

DATE STARTED: _____   DATE FINISHED: _____

MY REVIEW: _____

_____

Martin's Big Words: The Life of Dr. Martin Luther King, Jr.,
written by Doreen Rappaport, illustrated by Bryan Collier

Dr. Martin Luther King, Jr., was a man with a dream. He used his words to imagine a better world than the one he lived in. Read them and be inspired!

DATE STARTED: _____   DATE FINISHED: _____

MY REVIEW: _____

_____

Me on the Map, written by Joan Sweeney, illustrated by Annette Cable

Compared to the earth, we are all teeny tiny! That's why we use maps—to break it down into smaller sections: your room, your house, your street. Learn to map your world!

DATE STARTED: _____ DATE FINISHED: _____

MY REVIEW: _____

_____

Separate Is Never Equal, by Duncan Tonatiuh

In the 1940s, Sylvia Mendez was told that she couldn't go to the better school in town because it was only for white children. She knew this wasn't right, but what could she and her family do? Read about how they take action.

DATE STARTED: _____ DATE FINISHED: _____

MY REVIEW: _____

_____

Swing! by Rufus Butler Seder

A swimmer cuts through the water; a skater pirouettes on ice. Watch your favorite sports come to life before your eyes in this cool "scanimation" book!

DATE STARTED: _____ DATE FINISHED: _____

MY REVIEW: _____

_____

What Do You Do with a Tail Like This? by Steve Jenkins and Robin Page

Have you ever wondered why elephants have such long trunks? This book will answer all your questions about funny animal body parts!

DATE STARTED: _____ DATE FINISHED: _____

MY REVIEW: _____

_____

Wild Ideas, written by Elin Kelsey, illustrated by Soyeon Kim

Watch how animals solve problems, survive, and thrive! Read about how chimps fold leaves into cups or how a mimic octopus masters make-believe.

DATE STARTED: _____ DATE FINISHED: _____

MY REVIEW: _____

_____

And don't stop here! There's a whole world to discover. All you need is a book!

Summer Brain Quest
Mini Deck

QUESTIONS

What shape is on the top of the sand castle?

Which of these objects can roll down a hill?

QUESTIONS

Name the objects in the pictures. Which words rhyme?

Is the American flag at the top or bottom of the pole?

QUESTIONS

There were 7 balloons. One balloon hit a cactus and popped! How many balloons are left?

Which animal began as a caterpillar: a butterfly or a spider?

QUESTIONS

I like to chase mice, and my name rhymes with rat. What am I?

What color is the water on this globe?

ANSWERS

tree

bee

top

ANSWERS

cone

ANSWERS

cat

blue

ANSWERS

6 balloons

butterfly

QUESTIONS

If 5 monkeys are at a party, and 3 more monkeys join, how many monkeys will there be?

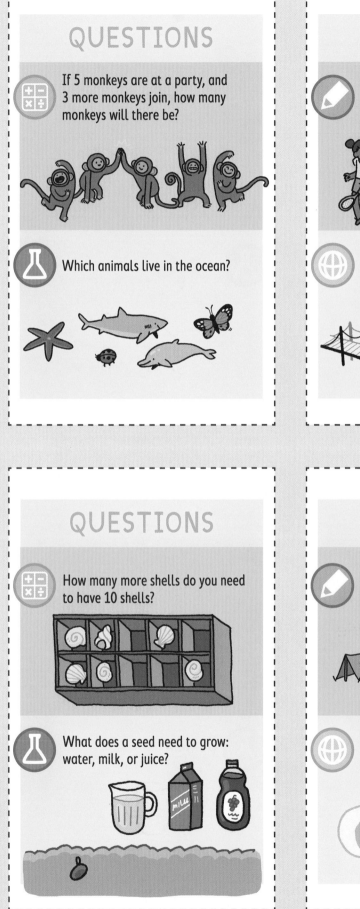

Which animals live in the ocean?

QUESTIONS

Find the noun in this sentence: **The ball flew quickly.**

Name the objects in the pictures. Which do you use to cross a river?

QUESTIONS

How many more shells do you need to have 10 shells?

What does a seed need to grow: water, milk, or juice?

QUESTIONS

Name the objects in the pictures. Which would you take camping?

Name the objects in the pictures. Which do you see at night?

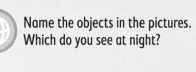

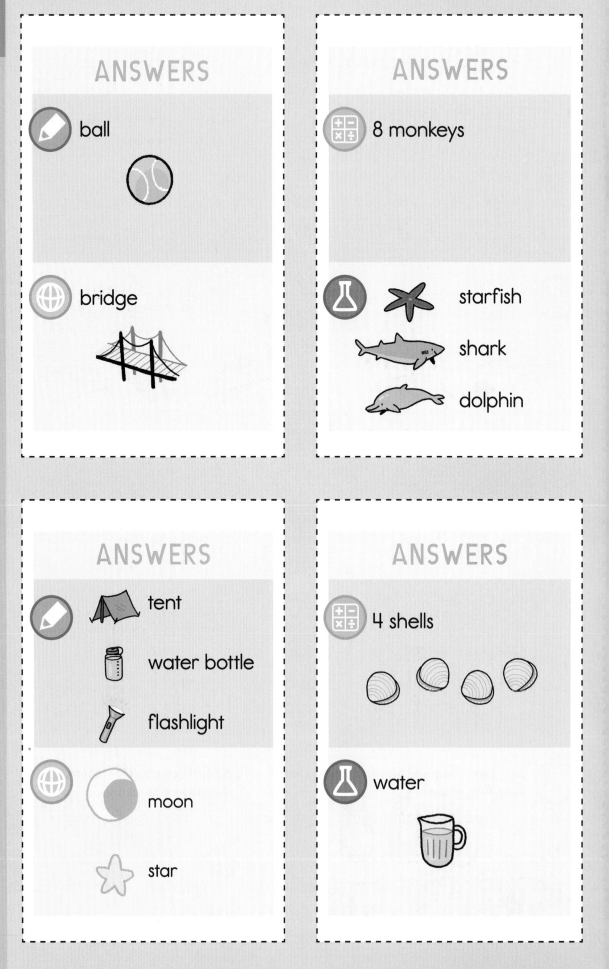

ANSWERS

- ball
- bridge

ANSWERS

- 8 monkeys
- starfish
- shark
- dolphin

ANSWERS

- tent
- water bottle
- flashlight
- moon
- star

ANSWERS

- 4 shells
- water

Summer Brain Quest: Between Grades K & 1

QUESTIONS

There are 7 butterflies. If 4 butterflies fly away, how many butterflies will be left?

Which of these animals grows into a frog?

QUESTIONS

What is the opposite of being asleep?

This doctor helps keep your teeth clean and healthy. What is this doctor called?

QUESTIONS

How many green triangles are shown?

Which instrument can be used to see things that are far away?

QUESTIONS

Choose the verb in this sentence: **The pilot flew the plane.**

Which color on a traffic light means stop?

ANSWERS

✏️ awake

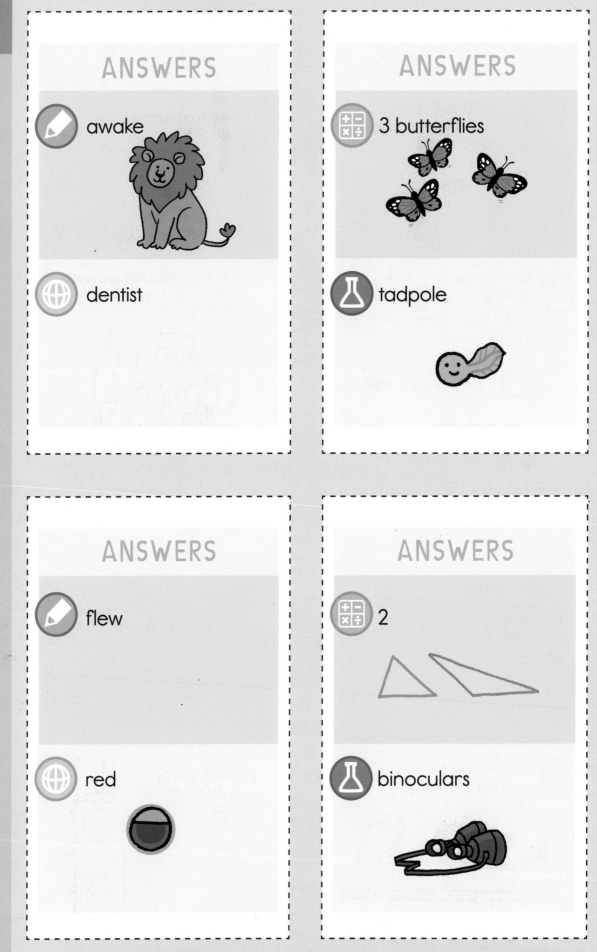

🌐 dentist

ANSWERS

🧮 3 butterflies

🧪 tadpole

ANSWERS

✏️ flew

🌐 red

ANSWERS

🧮 2

🧪 binoculars